Bible Study for
Young Adults
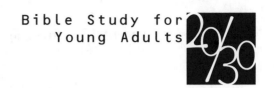

AFTERLIFE
Finding Hope Beyond Death

David deSilva

D1417045

Abingdon Press
Nashville

Afterlife: Finding Hope Beyond Death
20/30: Bible Study for Young Adults

by David deSilva

ISBN 0-687-05284X

This book is printed on acid-free paper.

MANUFACTURED IN THE UNITED STATES OF AMERICA

03 04 05 06 07 08 09 10 11 12—10 9 8 7 6 5 4 3 2 1

CONTENTS

MEET THE WRITER

DAVID DESILVA serves as Professor of New Testament and Greek at Ashland Theological Seminary, Ashland, Ohio. He is also ordained as a probationary member of the Florida Annual Conference of The United Methodist Church.

David has written twelve books including *Honor, Patronage, Kinship, and Purity: Unlocking New Testament Culture; Perseverance in Gratitude: A Commentary on the Epistle to the Hebrews; Praying With John Wesley; Paul and the Macedonians* in The Life and Letters of Paul series; and *Introducing the Apocrypha: Message, Context, and Significance.* He is currently completing an introduction to the New Testament for InterVarsity Press. He has also contributed to *Linktionary, Adult Bible Studies Teacher,* and Abingdon's line of music publications.

David, his wife, Donna Jean, and their three sons, Adrian, Austin, and Alexander, reside in Ashland. They attend Christ United Methodist Church, where Donna Jean volunteers in the area of Christian education, and David serves as organist and choir director.

WELCOME TO 20/30:
BIBLE STUDY
FOR YOUNG ADULTS

The *20/30* Bible study series is offered for postmodern adults who want to help structure their own discoveries—in life, in relationships, in faith. In each of the volumes of this series, you will have the opportunity to use your personal experiences in life and faith to examine the biblical texts in new ways. Each session offers biblical themes and images that have the power to shape contemporary human life.

The Power of Images

An image has evocative power. You can see, hear, smell, taste, and touch the image in your imagination. It also has the power to evoke memory and to inform ideas and feelings. Placing Christmas ornaments on a tree evokes memories of past Christmas celebrations or of circumstances surrounding the acquisition of the ornament. As an adult you may remember making the ornament as a gift for your mother, father, or another important person in your life. You may experience once again all the feelings you had when you gave this gift.

An image also informs and gives shape to themes and ideas such as hope, faith, love, and compassion. The image of the ornament gives a particular shape to love because each Christmas someone carefully places it on the tree. Love becomes specific and easy to identify.

Biblical Images

The Bible offers an array of powerful and evocative images through stories, parables, poems, proverbs, and sermons. Jesus used a variety of familiar images: a woman seeking a lost coin, a merchant finding a pearl, seeds and plants, and cups that are clean on the outside but dirty on the inside. Such images transcend time and place and speak to people today. A story about a Samaritan who helped a wounded person says far more than the simple assertion that loving a neighbor means *being* a neighbor. Each of the volumes in this series connects familiar, contemporary experiences with scriptural content through a shared knowledge of theme and image.

Power: Using or Abusing Our Potential
Mystery: Experiencing the Mystery of God
Grace: Being Loved, Loving God
Balance: Living With Life's Demands
Abundance: Living Responsibly With God's Gifts
Love: Opening Your Heart to God and Others
Faith: Living a Spirited Life
Covenant: Making Commitments That Count
Exodus: Leaving Behind, Moving On
Community: Living Faithfully With Others

Experience, Faith, Growth, and Action

Each volume in this series is designed to help you explore ways in which your experience links with your faith, and how deepening your faith expands your life experiences. As a prompt for reflection, each volume has several real-life case studies. Ways to be involved in specific service opportunities are listed on pages 77-78. Activities in each session suggest ways to engage you or a group with the themes and images in the Bible.

A core Christian belief affirms that God's graceful presence and activity moves through all creation. This series is designed to support your encounters with God in a community of faith through Scripture, reflection, and dialogue. One goal of such encounters is to enhance your individual and shared commitment to serve others in the hope that they too might experience God's graceful presence.

HOW TO USE THIS RESOURCE

Each session of this resource includes similar components or elements:
- a statement of the issue or question to be explored
- several "voices" of persons who are currently dealing with that issue
- exploration of biblical passages relating to the question raised
- "Bible 101" boxes that provide insight about the study of the Bible
- questions for reflection and discussion
- suggested individual and group activities designed to bring the session to life
- optional case studies (found in the back of the book)
- various service learning activities related to the session (found in the back of the book)

Choices, Choices, Choices

Collectively, these components mean one thing: *choice.* You have choices to make concerning how to use each session of this resource. Want just the nitty-gritty Bible reading, reflection, and study for personal or group use? Then focus your attention on just those components during your study time.

Like starting with real-life stories about issues then moving into how the Bible might be relevant? Start with the "voices" and move on from there. Use the "voices" to encourage group members to speak about their own experiences.

Prefer highly charged discussion encounters where many different viewpoints can be heard? Start the session with the biblical passages, followed by the questions and group activities. Be sure to compare the ideas found in the "Bible 101" boxes with your current ideas for more discussion. Want the major challenge of applying biblical principles to a difficult problem? After reading the biblical material, read one of the case studies, using the guidelines provided on page 14; or get involved with one of the service learning options described on pages 77-78.

Great Versatility

This resource has been designed for many different uses. Some persons will use this resource for personal study and reflection. Others will want to explore the work with a small group of friends. And still others will see this book as a different type of Sunday school resource.

Spend some time thinking about your own questions, study habits, and learning styles or those of your small group. Then use the guidelines mentioned above to fashion each session into a unique Bible study session to meet those requirements.

Highly Participatory

As you will see, the Scriptures, "voices," commentary, and experiences of group members will provide an opportunity for an active, engaging time together. The greatest challenge for a group leader might be "crowd control" —being sure everyone has the chance to put his or her ideas into the mix!

The Scriptures will help you and those who study with you to make connections between real-life issues and the Bible. This resource values and encourages personal participation as a means to understand fully and appreciate the intersection of personal belief with God's ongoing work in each and every life.

ORGANIZING A GROUP

Learning with a small group of persons offers certain advantages over studying by yourself. First, you will hopefully encounter different opinions and ideas, making the experience of Bible study a richer and more challenging event. Second, any leadership responsibilities can be shared among group members. Third, different persons will bring different talents. Some will be deep thinkers while other group members will be creative giants. Some persons will be newcomers to the Bible; their questions and comments will help others clarify their deeply held assumptions.

So how does one go about forming a small group? Follow the steps below and see how easy this task can be.

- **Read through the resource carefully.** Think about the ideas presented, the questions raised, and the exercises suggested. If the sessions of this work excite you, it will be easier for you to spread your enthusiasm to others.

- **Spend some time thinking about church members, friends, and coworkers who might find the sessions of this resource interesting**. On a sheet of paper, list two characteristics or talents you see in each person that would make him or her an attractive Bible study group member. Some talents might include "deep thinker," "creative wizard," or "committed Christian." Remember: The best small group has members who differ in learning styles, talents, ideas, and convictions, but who respect the dignity and integrity of the other members.

- **Most functional small groups have seven to fifteen members.** Make a list of potential group members that doubles your target number. For instance, if you would like a small group of seven to ten members, be prepared to invite fourteen to twenty persons.

- **Once your list of potential candidates is complete, decide on a tentative location and time.** Of course, the details can be negotiated with those persons who accept the invitation, but you need to sound definitive and clear to perspective group members. "We will initially set Wednesday night from 7 to 9 P.M. at my house for our meeting time" will sound more attractive than "Well, I don't know either when or where we would be meeting, but I hope you will consider joining us."

- **Make initial contact with prospective group members short, sweet, and to the point.** Say something like, "We are putting together a Bible study using a different kind of resource. When would be a good time to show you the resource and talk about the study?" Establishing a special time to make the invitation takes the pressure off the prospective group member to make a quick decision.

- **Show up at the decided time and place.** Talk with each prospective member individually. Bring a copy of the resource with you. Show each person what excites you about the study and mention the two unique characteristics or talents you feel he or she would offer the group. Tell each person the initial meeting time and location and how many weeks the small group will meet. Also mention that the need for a new time or location could be discussed during the first group meeting. Ask for a commitment to come to the first session. Thank individuals for their time.

- **Give a quick phone call or e-mail to thank all persons for their consideration and interest.** Remind persons of the time and location of the first meeting.

- **Be organized.** Use the first group meeting to get acquainted. Briefly describe the seven sessions. Have a book for each group member, and discuss sharing responsibilities for leadership.

PREPARING TO LEAD

So the responsibility to lead the group has fallen upon you? Don't sweat it. Follow these simple suggestions and not only will you prepare to lead, you will also find that your mind and heart are open to encounter the Christ who is with you.

- **Pray.** Find a quiet place. Have your Bible, the *20/30* book, paper, and pen handy. Ask for God's guidance and inspiration as you prepare for the session.

- **Read.** Look up all the Bible passages. Take careful notes about the ideas, statements, questions, and activities in the session. Jot down ideas and insights that occur to you as you read.

- **Think about group members.** Which ones like to think about ideas, concepts, or problems? Which ones need to "feel into" an idea by storytelling, worship, prayer, or group activities? Which ones are the "actors" who prefer a hands-on or participatory approach? Which ones might help you lead the session? Pray for each of the persons.

- **Think about the learning area and supplies.** What might you do with the place where you meet in order to enhance the experiences and activities of the session? Make a list of things such as poster paper, pens or pencils, paper, markers, large white paper, supplies for more creative activities, Bibles, music, hymnals, or any other supplies you might need for the activities in the session.

- **Think about special arrangements.** You may need to make special arrangements: inviting a guest speaker, planning an activity that occurs outside the regular time and place, or acquiring audiovisual equipment, for example.

- **Pray.** After you have thought through all the steps listed above, thank God for insights and inspiration about leading the group.

Using the Activity Icons

20/30 volumes include activity boxes marked with icons or images that indicate the kind of activity described in the box. The icons are intended to help you make decisions about which activities will best meet the needs of your group.

Start. A get-acquainted activity that introduces the focus of the session.

 Discuss. Activities designed to stimulate large group discussion.

 Small Group. Activities designed to stimulate discussion and reflection in groups of two or three persons. See the section "Using Break-out Groups" on pages 15-16.

 Bible. A Bible study activity that lists specific Scriptures. Participants will use the Bible.

 Look Closer. An activity designed to promote deeper, reflective awareness for an individual or for a group. The activity may call for use of resources such as Bible dictionaries or commentaries.

 Create. An activity designed for using a variety of creative art forms: drawing, sculpting, creating a mobile or a collage, or writing a poem or story.

 Case Study. An activity designed to explore and discuss a unique case study related to the session content or one of the case studies included in the back of the book.

 Serve. An activity that invites the group to discuss and engage in service to others. May relate directly to session content or to one of the service options in the back of the book.

 Music. An activity that uses music. May invite listening to a CD or singing a hymn, for example.

 Close. A closing activity that invites worship, celebration, or commitment to some specific action as a result of experiencing the session.

CHOOSING TEACHING OPTIONS

This young adult series was designed, written, and produced out of an understanding of the attributes, concerns, joys, and faith issues of young adults. With great care and integrity, this image-based print resource was developed to connect biblical events and relationships with contemporary, real-life situations of young adults. Its pages will promote Christian relationships and community, support new biblical learning, encourage spiritual development, and empower faithful decision-making and action.

This study is well-suited to young adults and may be used confidently and effectively. But with the great diversity within the young adult population, not every line of this study will be written "just for you." To be most relevant, some portions of the study material need to be tailored to fit your particular group. Adjustments for a good fit involve making choices from options offered by the resource. This customizing may be done easily by a designated leader who is familiar with the layout of the resource and the young adults who are using it.

What to Expect

In this study, Scripture and real-life images mesh together to provoke a personal response. Young adults will find themselves thinking, feeling, imagining, questioning, making decisions, professing faith, building connections, inviting discipleship, taking action, and making a difference. Scripture is at the core of each session. Scenarios weave in the dimensions of real life. Narrative and text boxes frame plenty of teaching options to offer young adults.

Each session is part of a cohesive volume, but it is also designed to stand alone. One session is not dependent on knowledge or experience accumulated from other sessions. A group leader can freely choose from the teaching options in an individual session without wondering about how it might affect the other sessions.

A Good Fit

For a better fit, alter the session based on what is known about the young adult participants. Young adults are a diverse constituency with varied experiences, interests, needs, and values. There is really no single defining characteristic that links young adults. Specific information about the age, employment status, household, personal relationships, and lifestyle among participants will equip a leader to make choices that ensure a good fit.

■ **Customize.** Read through the session. Notice how scenarios and teaching options move from integrating Scripture and real-life dimensions to inviting a response.

■ **Look at the scenario(s).** How real is the presentation of real life? Say that the main character is a professional, white male, married, in his early twenties, and caught in a workplace dilemma that entangles his immediate superior and a subordinate from his division. Perhaps your group members are mostly college students and recent graduates, unmarried, and still on the way to being "settled." There are many differences between the man in the scenario and these group members.

As a leader you could choose to eliminate the case study, substitute it with another scenario (there are several more choices on pages 76-78), claim the validity of the dilemma and shift the spotlight from the main character to the subordinate, or modify the description of the main character. Break-out groups based on age or employment experience might also be used to accommodate the differences and offer a better fit.

■ **Look at the teaching options.** How are the activities propelling participants toward a personal response? Perhaps the Scripture study requires more meditative quiet than is possible and a more academic, verbal, or artistic approach would offer a better fit. Maybe more direct decisions or actions would fit better than more passive or logical means. Try to keep a balance, though, that allows participants to "get out of their head" to reflect and also to move toward action.

Conceivably, there could be too much in any one session. As a leader, you can pick and choose among teaching options, substitute case studies, take two meetings to do one session, and adapt any process to make a better fit. The tailoring process can be evaluated as adjustments are made. Judge the fit every time you meet. Ask questions that gauge relevance, and assess how the resource has stretched minds, encouraged discipleship, and changed lives.

USING BREAK-OUT GROUPS

20/30 break-out groups are small groups that encourage the personal sharing of lives and the gospel. The word *break-out* is a sweeping term that includes a variety of small group settings. A break-out group may resemble a Bible study group, an interest group, a sharing group, or other types of Christian fellowship groups.

Break-out groups offer young adults a chance to belong and personally relate to one another. Members are known, nurtured, and heard by others. Young adults may agree and disagree while maximizing the exchange of ideas, information, or options. They might explore, confront, and resolve personal issues and feelings with empathy and support. Participants can challenge and hold one another accountable to a personalized faith and stretch its links to real life and service.

Forming Break-out Groups

As you look through this book you will see an icon that says "Small Group." The nature of these small break-out groups will depend on the context and design of the specific session. On occasion the total group of participants will be divided for a particular activity. Break-out groups will differ from one session to the next. Variations may involve the size of the group, how group members are divided, or the task of the group. Break-out groups may also be used to accommodate differences and help tailor the session plan for a better fit. In some sessions, specific group assembly instructions will be provided. For other sessions, decisions regarding the size or division of small groups will be made by the designated leader. Break-out groups may be in the form of pairs or trios, family-sized groups of three to six members, or groups of up to ten members.

They may be arranged simply by grouping persons seated next to one another or in more intentional ways by common interests, characteristics, or life experience. Consider creating break-out groups according to age; gender; type of household, living arrangements, or love relationships; vocation, occupation, career, or employment status; common or built-in connections; lifestyle; values or perspective; or personal interests or traits.

Membership

The membership of break-out groups will vary from session to session, or even within specific sessions. Young adults need to work at knowing and being known, so that there can be a balance between break-out groups that

15

are more similar and those that reflect greater diversity. There may be times when more honest communication, trust, or accountability may be desired and group leaders will need to be free to self-select members for small groups.

It is important for *20/30* break-out groups to practice acceptance and to value the worth of others. The potential for small groups to encourage personal sharing and significant relationships is enhanced when members agree to exercise active listening skills, keep confidences, expect authenticity, foster trust, and develop ways of loving one another. All group members contribute to the development and function of break-out groups. Designated leaders especially need to model manners of hospitality and help ensure that each group member is respected.

Invitational Listening

Consider establishing an "invitational listening" routine that validates the perspective and affirms the voice of each group member. After a question or statement is posed, pause and allow time to think—not all persons think on their feet or talk out loud to think. Then, initiate conversation by inviting one group member, by name, to talk. This person may either choose to talk or to "pass." Either way, this person is honored and is offered an opportunity to speak and to be heard. This person carries on the ritual by inviting another group member, by name, to speak. The process continues until all have been invited, by name, to talk. As each one invites another, the responsibility of acceptance and hospitality in the break-out groups is shared among all its members.

Study group members break-out to belong, to share the gospel, to care, and to watch over one another in Christian love. "So deeply do we care for you that we are determined to share with you not only the gospel of God but also our own selves, because you have become very dear to us" (1 Thessalonians 2:8).

AFTERLIFE:
FINDING HOPE BEYOND DEATH

What happens when I die? Is death the end of me? Is there more than this life? We share many functions with the animals; the ability to reflect on our own mortality and seek meaning and hope in the face of death, as far as we can tell, is a particular function of human beings. This ability is a particularly important function. The extent to which we can come to terms with our own death directly impacts our psychological stability and well-being. The denial of death leads to all manner of personality disorders and ultimately to an insecure, inauthentic life.

The gospel of Jesus Christ brings good news in the face of death. When God raised Jesus from the dead, God confirmed the hope of pious Jews that those who died faithful to God would experience God's faithfulness beyond death. Jesus' resurrection foreshadows our own resurrection, proclaims the hope of life in the presence of God forever, and invites us now to live in and for this hope. God's triumph over death extends beyond our individual lives as well, to the redemption of human community and creation itself, freeing all creation from the forces of death and decay at work now.

It is impossible to resolve all the mysteries of death and the life beyond death—and the mysteries of God's interventions in life, death, and beyond—into a neat system. We are looking "in a mirror, dimly" (1 Corinthians 13:12), like the biblical witnesses themselves. Still their witness points us to strong hope and the possibility of a life freed from "slavery by the fear of death" (Hebrews 2:15).

A Matter of Life as Well as Death

Exploring questions about death and the life beyond also brings new perspectives on, and insights into, the life we are now living. The fact of death on its own has much to teach us about living wisely and meaningfully in the time that we have. What do we make our priorities during our time here? To what pursuits will we give our limited time? When we wrestle seriously with death, we are wrestling with "ultimate" things, not only in the sense of "last" things but also in the sense of "most important," "most valuable," "most real" things.

The Christian hope of life beyond death, of embarking now upon a journey that leads to endless life, invites us to look very closely and critically at the forces at work in our lives. Do we contribute to the forces of death at work in the world, dragging us, our fellow human beings, our environment, down to decay and death? Or, turning away from death-dealing patterns of relating and acting, do we work to affirm what is healthful and life-giving for all humanity?

As we consider how we weigh the alternatives set before us in this life, will we live as if we are ultimately accountable to no one, or as if there is an ultimate standard for life in human community to which we are accountable? Are the choices we make, the values we embody, the pursuits we choose ultimately irrelevant and trivial, or are they dignified with great moral significance beyond our mortal lives? Looking at our lives from the vantage point of eternity can empower many triumphs over temptation to be less of a discipline than we would wish. It can also enbolden us to witness courageously to our society, challenging it to become the community of life, peace, and justice that God would wish. Finally, it can give us the gift of living our lives with integrity, so that, when we face death and stand at the threshold of eternity, we shall face it without regrets.

The best discoveries about the biblical witness to "life beyond death" will be made as you test them out in your life and experience. The validation will come as you step forward in the insights you will gain.

A Note About Resources

In the course of this journey, you will be invited to read several selections from books contained in the Old Testament Apocrypha. Jewish convictions about the afterlife really blossomed during the period between the Old and New Testaments, and so it is of special importance to include those witnesses in a study of this kind. Texts such as the Wisdom of Solomon (written by a pious Jew in the first century B.C.) or Second Maccabees (written in the late second or early first century B.C.) give us important windows into the developing thought world of Judaism and therefore provide important background for what we find in the New Testament. When reading the Apocrypha, we should bear in mind that the majority of the world's Christians regard these as part of the Old Testament and hence part of the spiritual heritage of the church. Protestants have historically not regarded them as of equal value to the Old and New Testaments. Nevertheless, many Reformation-era leaders still commended the Apocrypha as edifying literature for the Christian to read and ponder. You will therefore want to have access to a Bible containing the Apocrypha or at least a separate edition of the Apocrypha.

LIVING IN THE SHADOW OF DEATH

This session looks at the ways in which people respond to their mortality, either healthfully in ways that lead to a richer life or in ways that contribute to inauthentic living.

GETTING STARTED

"Two things are certain in this life: death and taxes." The cliché is half right. Death is the defining fact of our existence. We are mortal, and we must die. Before we can talk meaningfully about an afterlife, we need to be able to talk bravely about our own deaths and the significance of death for the way we live our lives here and now.

This is a difficult subject for many people. We tend to deny our own mortality, to block from view our own death and dying. This is mirrored in the way we treat other people who are dying and the bodies that remain after death. Death is the elephant in the living room that no one wants to talk about.

Christian faith does not join in the silence and avoidance of death, however. Our traditions and Scriptures encourage us to face our anxiety about death rather than to repress that anxiety. This is healthful

Getting Started
Introduce yourselves to one another if the group is new or if new people have joined. Reflect on these questions: In what ways have you encountered death? In what ways have you been confronted with and dealt with the fact of your own mortality? What did you learn from these experiences?

because anything that is repressed tends to take control of our lives below the conscious level, enslaving us, in effect. The first work of liberation that the gospel enables begins here.

MONICA AND JANELLE

Janelle: Hey Monica, did your uncle ever get the results from his tests?

Monica: Yes. The doctors said it was pancreatic cancer. He's got about two months.

Janelle: Monica, I'm so sorry. Have you gone to see him?

Monica: I've thought about it, but I'm really swamped. Can't seem to get away. Besides, I don't really know what to say to him.

Janelle: Two years ago my great-aunt died. We were really close. I went to see her a few times. She was just glad for the company, to know I cared.

Monica: Yes, well, my uncle's only forty. It's like a death sentence to be told you have cancer so young.

Janelle: It could happen to anyone at any age. Best thing to do is to live in such a way that, whenever it comes, we have no regrets.

Monica: You're really fun today. I'd love to chat, but I've got to finish this report before five.

AN END, IF NOT THE END

People throughout history have wrestled with the meaning of death and what it means for human life. Ideas of afterlife are present in virtually every culture. However, many cultures have also reckoned with the possibility that death is, in some sense, an absolute end. Many voices from Scripture even speak of death as the absolute endpoint of personal existence. Job contrasts a dead tree that might put forth new life again with the human being who dies and will never revive (Job 14:7-12). He figuratively wishes that God would temporarily hide him in the grave, so that God would no longer take notice of his sin (verses 13-17); but this is a wish he himself cannot sustain (verses 18-22).

The psalmists also speak of the grave as not only an end to human consciousness, and thus their remembrance and praise of God, but also an end of God's remembrance of people (Psalms 6:4-5; 30:8-9; 88:3-5, 10-12). One of the greatest horrors about death seems to be that it puts people beyond the reach of God's help—if God does not restore health or bring help before death, is there anything God can do for the person after death?

STRANGELY UNNATURAL

If you have ever stood near an open casket at a wake, you have probably heard someone remark about the corpse, "He looks so natural" or "She looks so natural." While this might delight the undertaker's staff of cosmeticians, it also raises the question, is there anything natural about a dead body?

From a biological point of view, death is a natural process. The organism comes to its appointed and biologically defined end, having run its course, having gone through a process of winding down, and having ceased to function. Nevertheless, there are also many indications that death is regarded as decidedly unnatural.

Bible 101: The Intrusion of Death

The Genesis story is not entirely clear about the place of death in God's creation. Death is mentioned as the consequence of trangressing the limits God placed on humanity (Genesis 2:15-17), but does this mean that humanity was created immortal or that God would merely bring their death upon them more swiftly? (Immortality seems not to be inherent in Genesis 3:22-24). Later readers definitely decided in favor of death being an unnatural intrusion into God's purposes for creation. Death is not part of the natural processes inherent in creation from the beginning, hence a "good" and "natural" experience (1:31) but marks a departure from God's intentions for creation, a result of creation being "out of sync" with God and God's life-giving ways.

The Wisdom of Solomon was written in the first century B.C. and appears in the Old Testament Apocrypha. (See "Afterlife: Finding Hope Beyond Death" on page 17.) The author of this book says explicitly that "God did not make death" (Wisdom of Solomon 1:13), but rather created people to be righteous and to enjoy immortality: "God created us for incorruption, / and made us in the image of his own eternity" (2:23).

Death is something humanity summoned for itself. Paul stands firmly within this stream of thought. For him, death is linked with sin and rebellion against God (Romans 1:29-32), entering human experience in general—and each person's experience in particular—through disobedience (Romans 5:12-21; 6:20-23).

Both authors, however, also speak of God having made provisions yet to fulfill God's purposes for us, extending the hope of entering into a life beyond death through aligning ourselves now with righteousness.

BIBLE

Read Genesis 1:26-31; 2:15-17; 3:1-7, 17-19, 22-24. What is the place of death in God's creation?

Read Romans 5:12-21; 6:20-23 and Wisdom of Solomon 1:12-15; 2:22-24. What were God's purposes for humanity, and how did death invade history? What do these texts say about the unnaturalness of death and about the kind of life that is considered to be natural for us?

ADAM'S STORY, OUR STORY

Even though Adam is traditionally blamed for the invasion of human life by sin and death, James is aware that each of us becomes his or her own Adam, repeating that story in our own lives (James 1:14-16). Adam and Eve represent humanity trying to do an end-run around God to secure their own divinity and immortality apart from a relationship of absolute trust in God, God's words, and God's goodness. After all, the snake achieved victory by convincing Eve that God was withholding good from them and lying about the consequences just to "keep them down."

We see forbidden delights, fear that an antiquated morality is trying to repress us, and gratify our desires under the banner of "self-realization." We hear God's promises but also think to ourselves that if we are going to make it, we are going to have to make it on our own.

Death, however, is a boundary we cannot cross on our own; the fact of death forces us to learn this lesson. Death invites us to accept our own finitude and to receive life here and beyond as a gift from God and not as something we make for ourselves. This, in turn, opens up the path to authentic living, to freedom from the frenzied and useless attempts to insulate ourselves against death by which we actually lose ourselves and fill ourselves up merely with distractions from authentic living.

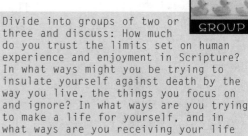

Divide into groups of two or three and discuss: How much do you trust the limits set on human experience and enjoyment in Scripture? In what ways might you be trying to insulate yourself against death by the way you live, the things you focus on and ignore? In what ways are you trying to make a life for yourself, and in what ways are you receiving your life as a gift from God? Where in all this do you experience anxiety or peace?

RUNNING AWAY FROM DEATH?

Scripture often compares human beings with the quickly blooming and withering wild flowers or insubstantial breath and shadows (Job 14:1-2; Psalm 39:4-6, 12-13; Isaiah 40:6-8). One prominent response to this realization, conscious or not, is to repress it beneath a frenzied attempt to enjoy all the good things this life can offer while there is still time. This response is masterfully portrayed in the Wisdom of Solomon 1:16–2:11.

The awareness that time is slipping away makes the people described here grasping,

What do you think makes for a satisfying life? What do you invest most of your time trying to accomplish or attain? To what extent are you investing your time and energies in those things you say are really valuable to you?

Running Away From Death?
Read Wisdom of Solomon 1:16–2:11. How do the people described there respond to the fact of their mortality? Does their activity fill their lives or leave them empty? Why do you think that? What are the social and relational consequences the author sees where people respond to mortality this way?

What commodities or pursuits promise a satisfying life but end up yielding an unsatisfying life? Make a collage of the kinds of goods and activities that you use, or at least are available for you to use, to distract yourself from ultimate issues.

STUDY   **Devon**
Read Devon's soliloquy. What does she consider life to be? How has she sought security in the face of death or insulation against disappearing like the biblical mist, shadow, or grass? What has she sacrificed? Has Devon really given her life substance, or is she courting the danger of losing herself in the attempt to gain the whole world?

acquisitive, fearful that the "good things" and pleasures of life might pass them by. They do not remain centered and grounded; as a result, they betray the ethics learned from their heritage, their covenant relationships with God and with one another, and ultimately themselves. They do not combine an awareness of death with a hope for life beyond death. They do not perceive God to be at work behind the mysteries of life and of death. In effect, this wholly naturalistic view of life and death leads to an ethic of self-gratification and predation on others. The outcomes of their beliefs are simply not satisfactory, since we have all experienced (or at least suspected) the emptiness of the pursuits upon which they settle.

DEVON

Finally, everything's paying off. In college and law school, I worked through breaks and weekends to be among the top of my class. I hustled as a paralegal to get the attention of the partners and finally got a break to start trying cases. Working sixty- to seventy-hour weeks, I established an impeccable court record and finally made partner; and I did it all on my own.

Of course there were costs. My husband didn't value the sacrifices that had to be made to get to the top, even though I brought in enough money to ensure that we had a great home, the best cars, the sharpest image. I haven't seen my sister's child yet, and he's almost two. I've had to learn a lot about the real world and let go of my childish idealism; but you've got to give it your all and play the game if you're going to get anywhere and be somebody in this world. Now I've made it. I'm here to stay.

LEARNING ABOUT LIFE IN THE SCHOOL OF DEATH

The traditional funeral mass included a reading of Psalm 90:12: "So teach us to count our days / that we may gain a wise heart." Our spiritual ancestors understood that looking our own death straight in the face was a road to living well, to shaping a life without regrets. Medieval and Renaissance paintings of saints and scholars often show a skull sitting on the desk of the wise person alongside his or her books. Contemplation of their end, these paintings say, contributed to making the sage wise. Stopping from the busy-ness—the endless stream of distraction from ultimate questions—to consider our own mortality could teach us much about spending life well.

THE BEST LAID PLANS

Adam and Eve learned the hard way that they were not God. James would have us keep in mind the fact that we are not ultimately the masters of our own destinies when we make plans for ourselves (James 4:13-17). All our short- and long-range planning comes to pass solely at God's discretion. To forget that we are finite and dependent is arrogance and even sin.

WHAT AM I LIVING FOR?

Our own mortality tells us something about the value of the many things we pursue as if our life depended on it. If we invest in those things that pass away with us—our self-indulgent desires, our grasping for material goods, our pride in our livelihood

(1 John 2:15-17)—we will have lost both our principal and its dividends. The fleeting nature of life should impel us all the more toward spending our lives doing something that will have an impact beyond our own enjoyment and security.

INVESTING WISELY

"You can't take it with you." More than a cliché, this is precisely the lesson of the Bible concerning wealth (Psalm 49:17; Luke 12:13-21; 1 Timothy 6:7). The fact of death counsels us not to be taken in by the society's tendency to speak of a person's net worth in dollar amounts, because in any ultimate sense this will have nothing to do with his or her real worth.

Luke offers us a story about a rich man who was occupied only with making more money and finding better places to store his hoard. On his deathbed, he is confronted with the real poverty of his soul (Luke 12:13-21). Jesus reminds us in Matthew that a rich life consists of more than food, clothing, abundance of possessions; it means pursuing God's kingdom and God's justice (Matthew 6:19-21, 25-33). Death poses for us the agenda of learning how to be "rich toward God" (Luke 12:21).

The solemn facts of death lead to wisdom regarding the pursuit and use of this world's wealth, to prioritizing the pursuit of righteousness and discipleship as that which bears fruit that transcends death. Not security in wealth, but security in God avails in the face of death; not hoarding, but generous relief of those in need allows one to take hold of the life that really is life (1 Timothy 6:13), a reward that we begin to enjoy in the relationships we form thereby.

BIBLE

Investing Wisely
Read Luke 12:13-21, 32-34. How has the rich man deceived himself about life and security? To what extent do you identify with the rich man? Now read 1 Timothy 6:6-12, 17-19. How does that passage use the fact of our mortality to prioritize our ambitions for this life? How is the wise person to relate to the pursuit and accumulation of wealth? Where, and to what extent, do you find yourself mirrored in this text?

CLOSE

Close
Ask each group member: What was the most helpful insight you gained today? What do you feel led to re-examine about your life or to do? Pray for one another to treasure these insights and to follow God's leading.

26

THE GOD OF THE LIVING

This session explores the biblical teachings about the afterlife and what these teachings show about God's nature.

SHADOWY BEGINNINGS

The ancient Israelites had no developed concept of an afterlife. Rather, everyone simply went to the grave, to a shadowy existence in Sheol. The spirit of the dead entered into a vaguely defined post-mortem existence. They were believed to be available for consultation by mediums, as the many prohibitions of this activity indicate (Leviticus 19:31; 20:27; Deuteronomy 18:10-14; Isaiah 8:19-20).

The most famous "ghost story" of the Old Testament is found in 1 Samuel 28 in which Saul, in desperate need of guidance for his war against the Philistines, asks the medium at Endor to conjure up the spirit of the prophet Samuel, who had recently died. Samuel regards this as a disturbance perhaps of his rest, the unconsciousness of the dead in Sheol. The possibility, at least, of encoun-

Getting Started
Center your heart on God in a moment of silent prayer. Talk about ways in which you have nurtured the insights or responded to the challenges you took away from the previous session. Introduce any new members.

tering ghosts or spirits is attested in the New Testament as well (Mark 6:47-50).

WHO IS OUR GOD?

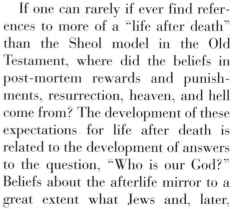

Shadowy Beginnings
Have you ever experienced, or known someone who experienced, the presence of a dead relative or friend? How did you respond to that event? What does it say to you about this life and about death?

Have you had, or known someone who had, a near-death or out-of-body experience? How do you explain such phenomena? What do such experiences tell us about our makeup as human beings? about the nature and dimensions of our lives?

If one can rarely if ever find references to more of a "life after death" than the Sheol model in the Old Testament, where did the beliefs in post-mortem rewards and punishments, resurrection, heaven, and hell come from? The development of these expectations for life after death is related to the development of answers to the question, "Who is our God?" Beliefs about the afterlife mirror to a great extent what Jews and, later, Christians came to understand and affirm about the character of God. If they were pressed to explain their hopes for, and understanding of, life after death, Jews and Christians from the first century would probably have answered, "Because God is whom God is."

A JUST GOD

A prominent characteristic of God celebrated in Scripture is God's justice or righteousness. God upholds those who do what is right and opposes those who do what is wrong. This message unifies the Law, the prophets, the wisdom literature, and the New Testament. The basic operating principle of Deuteronomy, exemplified from Joshua through First Kings, is that God will continue his favor toward those who uphold God's covenant, walking in the ways that God has laid

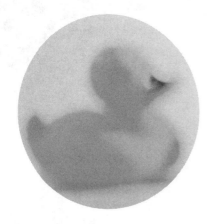

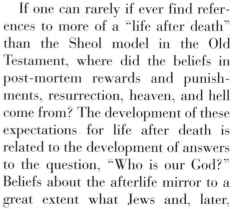

SMALL GROUP In groups of three, talk about the reasons you have to think that there is more to our existence than this life and why your beliefs in an afterlife take the form that they do. Also talk about what doubts you have about life and death and why you have them.

List the major factors behind beliefs in, or doubts about, an afterlife that came out of your small groups. Write these down on a chalkboard or a large sheet of paper. What trends emerge? Report the highlights of your discussion to the larger group.

out as righteous. Conversely, God will punish those who flout God's standards of righteousness, who break God's covenant. God acts justly in regard to the relationships he has formed and the obligations he has placed upon humanity in general and Israel in particular.

What happens, though, when those who faithfully keep God's commandments come to a bad end, while those who live heedless of God and God's law prosper in this life? Although it is true that goodness tends to be vindicated by history, and villainy and evil exposed, this does not happen with sufficient regularity within an individual's lifetime. How can God be just not only in general, but also specifically to each individual?

SEVEN BROTHERS

Between 166 and 164 B.C., the covenant loyalty of Jews was put to the supreme test. Because of ongoing unrest in Judea, Antiochus IV, the Greco-Syrian king, outlawed the observance of Jewish customs and practice. Jews who persisted in trying to keep the covenant with God (for example, through circumcision of their male children) were executed. A story is told of seven brothers who endured brutal torture rather than agree to leave the Mosaic covenant behind them (signified by their eating pork). All of them died horribly as a direct result of keeping the covenant, whereas God had promised blessings to those who kept the covenant.

They are remembered, however, as full of the hope for immortality and a renewed life

The God of the Living

in the presence of God as a reward
for their faithfulness. Trusting completely in God's just character, they
gave their lives for the covenant,
sure that God would give them
their lives back again and would in
turn punish the tyrant for merci-
lessly assaulting God's people
(2 Maccabees 7; see also 4 Maccabees
9:8-9, 32; 10:11, 15; 13:14-15;
15:3; 16:13; 17:12; Daniel 12:1-3,
which many scholars believe came from this
period as well). A clear hope for a life
beyond death and a differentiation between
the after-death existence of the obedient
and the wicked emerges most clearly in
relation to this crisis.

A LOVING AND FAITHFUL GOD

Another important characteristic of God
is God's love and reliability toward God's
people. A constant theme of Scripture is
that when God initiates a relationship, God
is absolutely faithful to those people with
whom God is in relationship. In the Old
Testament this is expressed mainly in
terms of covenant faithfulness
(*chesed*). Many things changed in the
situation and fortunes of Israel and
Judah, but God's covenant faithfulness
was seen to be constant, a foundation
of bedrock. It was natural, then, that
God's faithfulness and love would
come to be understood to transcend
even death (Romans 8:35-39). No force is
greater than God's love, no power greater
than God's reliability.

Paul also expresses this by speaking of
God's ownership of us in life and in death
(Romans 14:7-9). God has purchased, or

30

ransomed, us for God's self (1 Corinthians 6:19-20; Revelation 5:9-10) and so has brought us into a special relationship analogous to the covenant enjoyed by the ancient Israelites. Just as God showed covenant faithfulness to them, so Paul expects God to show the same unflinching, unwavering, undying faithfulness to the people God redeemed in Christ—thus, again, in life and in death.

Another angle on God's faithfulness emerges in the letter to the Hebrews, as the author thinks about the difficult story of Abraham's near-sacrifice of Isaac (Genesis 22:1-19). What would have allowed Abraham to be willing to kill his son? According to the author of Hebrews, Abraham's absolute assurance that God would be faithful to God's promises led to a firm conviction that God could raise Isaac from the dead (Hebrews 11:19).

A MIGHTY GOD

One of the first big theological words we probably learned was *omnipotent*, if only from singing the "Hallelujah Chorus" from the *Messiah* by Frederic Handel. "All things are possible with God" because God is a God of unlimited power. As people reflected on death, which they also held to be a great power in their world, the question about whether or not God has power over death naturally arose. Some of the psalms speak as if God's power and sphere of concern stop at the graveside. The author of Psalm 139:5-12, however, lost in the wonder and praise of God, declared that even the grave is not removed from God's presence. The author apparently came to

A Loving and Faithful God
Read Romans 8:35-39; 14:7-9; Hebrews 11:17-19. What convictions about God and God's way of relating to people are expressed in these passages? What is the connection between God's relational style and convictions about the power of death?

Sing (or read) the hymn "Abide With Me." What is happening to the speaker of these lyrics? What is of most importance to him or her in those circumstances? How does the writer help connect the themes of relationship, God's faithfulness, and hope for life beyond death?

A Mighty God
Read Romans 4:16-21, and 1 Corinthians 15:24-28. What is the faith of Abraham in Romans 4:16-21, and how does it relate to God's power in the face of death? What do both texts say about the power of death? What do the Scriptures say to you about your experience of God? When have you sensed God's power or witnessed it at work? In your experience, is death or God the more powerful force? Why?

see that the earlier vision of God was too small.

The God who "calls into existence the things that do not exist," a power exemplified most vividly in the Creation story, is also the God "who gives life to the dead" (Romans 4:17). Paul takes for granted God's power over death, finding it surprising, in fact, that others might *not* share this conviction (Acts 26:8). Such is God's power that it must eventually result in the complete banishment of death from God's good creation (1 Corinthians 15:24-28).

YOU WANT PROOF?

Scripture is full not only of affirmations of God's power over death, but also of examples of this power in action. In both testaments, people who died are raised to life again by God's power (1 Kings 17:8-24; Matthew 9:18-26; Luke 7:11-17; John 11). In the New Testament, these events are understood as signs that Jesus is a source of life for his followers, for this life and the life beyond death (John 6:21, 25-29; 11:21-27).

Those who came back to life from the dead, however, would die again. God's promise of life for those who trust and obey God extends to a life beyond the power of death, hence resurrection, a qualitatively different kind of life than the life of this mortal body (Hebrews 11:35, which contrasts the two kinds of life after death). The resurrection of Jesus from the dead gave a new, historical basis to the hope for life beyond death, beyond the theological basis found already in Judaism (as seen in Second Maccabees).

The result of these convictions about God and experiences of the risen Lord is that

BIBLE

You Want Proof?
Read the accounts of encountering the resurrected Jesus in Luke 24:15-16, 30-32; 36-43; and John 20:14-16, 19, 26-28. What do the texts say about a resurrected body? How is it like our mortal body? unlike our mortal body?

Sheol, the grave or underworld, is transformed from a permanent holding bin to the womb, as it were, of a pregnant woman. It grows with its increasing burden, but one day that burden will burst forth as the dead entrusted to the grave will one day be brought forth to a different life beyond the power of death (2 Esdras 4:40-42; Revelation 20:13).

RESURRECTION FAITH

Paul speaks much about learning to rely on the "God who raises the dead" in his second letter to the Corinthian Christians. The conviction that God will raise us from the dead—something we certainly cannot do by any power or giftedness of our own—challenges Paul and his churches to forgo a false faith or confidence rooted "on ourselves" (2 Corinthians 1:9).

Some rival missionaries, as well as many within Paul's congregation, were still caught up in putting on a good appearance, finding a ground for self-confidence and for evaluating other people in temporal strengths, worldly credentials, and panache. As long as people played that game, they would not discover the life-giving power of God. The realization of the limits of human power and the ultimate dependency we all share on God's power to bring us across the final threshold freed Paul to live out his faith in an authentic, transparent walk. No longer bound by the need to conceal his weaknesses and show a veneer of human strength, he was freed to look for, and thus provide a living example of, the

DISCUSS

In your own religious experience, what do you know about God's character? What are some absolute certainties? How have you come to know these things about God? How does this shape your orientation toward this life and your convictions about death and afterlife?

BIBLE

Resurrection Faith
Read 2 Corinthians 1:8-9; 3:4-6; 4:7-14; 12:6-10. How do you feel about letting your weaknesses show? What public face do you try to display so that other people will value you? Why would Paul place no value on human strengths but only on God's transforming presence? What role does the hope for life beyond death play in Paul's value judgments here?

working of God's power to transform him from within.

FREEDOM FROM SLAVERY

Freedom From Slavery
Read Hebrews 2:14-15. How might the fear of death enslave a person in destructive, limiting ways? How does Jesus' death bring us freedom, and how does this freedom affect our lives? If death is not the end, how am I freed to live now? How are the blinders taken off?

While the fear of death can keep us from doing many dumb things, it can also subtly affect the way we live and limit our willingness to respond to God's call. For fear of death, many bold witnesses for God and justice become cowards. For fear that life is slipping by them, many strong disciples turn their focus away from serving God and toward making a life for themselves.

Jesus died, in part, in order to free us from our enslavement by this fear (Hebrews 2:14-15), which was explored at length in Session One. If allowed to take hold in our lives, our convictions about God's ability to give life to the dead can reshape our whole approach to this life and give wind to the sails of our boldest visions for serving God's desires for the human community. Death remains a sobering reality but no longer a tyrant controlling and limiting how we live.

Sing or read the hymn "Easter People, Raise Your Voices." According to the poet, what changes has the resurrection of Jesus and the hope for our own resurrection brought to our orientation to this life? Where do you resonate with his words? Point out any lines that seem somewhat remote or like clichés.

TWO LIVES TO LIVE?

In light of the witness of the Scriptures, we are left to wonder if we should call our post-mortem existence an "*after*life" or consider the present time more of a "pre-life." The life beyond death, they declare, is ultimate and endless and thus the more real and weighty of the two. This creates its own investment strategies and priorities for this life, and generally they are found to be the more satisfactory for the here and now and for the hereafter.

Close
Read aloud John 11:25-26; 1 Corinthians 15:54-57; and Revelation 1:17b-18. Pray that God will reveal more and more of God's character to you, so that your hope will always be firmly rooted in your experience of God.

LIVING BEYOND DEATH

This session explores God's invitation to put death-bound ways behind us and to begin to enter into eternal life in the here and now.

AFTERLIFE?

The word *afterlife* suggests two things. First, *this* life is privileged as our principal life, the "norm." Whatever we experience beyond death is something *after* life is over, something secondary. Second, the term assumes clear-cut boundaries between the life we now experience and the afterlife into which we enter as a result of dying.

These suggestions run counter to the early Christian understanding of life and existence beyond death. Our present experience is secondary, the prelude to our ultimate experience of life in eternity and the fullness of God's presence. Moreover, we begin to enter into that experience of eternal life in the midst of this life. The writers of the New Testament regard physical death as the final stage in a process of transition that often begins long before. For them, entrance into the afterlife really begins

Getting Started
Sing or read the hymn "Because He Lives." What significance does the author of this text see in the death and resurrection of Jesus? How do these words resonate with your own experience? Where do they not? If you were to finish the sentence "Because He Lives," what would you write? Write the answers on a piece of newsprint or a chalkboard.

BIBLE

Afterlife?
Read 1 John 3:14; 5:11-12. What
do you think of the notion that
eternal life is something that begins only
after death? What does it mean to have
eternal life before death? What relationships do you see between the way we live
and the quality of life that we have
(whether death or life)? In what sense
might the Christian be said to have passed
from death to life long before actually
experiencing physical death?

SMALL

GROUP   **The Mystery of Faith**
Find a partner. Talk
about how you connect with the
story of Jesus' death and resurrection. How real is that
story for you? Why would New
Testament authors be so insistent that Jesus' death and
resurrection is not just *his*
story but provides the means
for us to experience a similar
victory over death? When and
how have you experienced that
level of connection with his
story?

when a person is born anew, or is joined with Christ, and proceeds as a person nurtures and lives out this new life that is made available in Christ.

From a New Testament perspective, it would be more appropriate to speak of the Christian hope in terms of living beyond death, a kind of living that we must begin to live before death if we expect to live after death.

THE MYSTERY OF FAITH

The biblical vision for living beyond death takes us to the central mystery of Christianity—the death and resurrection of Jesus. The good news is that we do not encounter death alone at the end of this life but that we can encounter it together with Jesus before our physical death, transforming the experience of death into an awakening to life. To the eyes of faith, Jesus' death is not merely the undeserved end of a revolutionary teacher, but a tasting of death on behalf of all people (Hebrews 2:9). It is, moreover, a prelude to his resurrection, an intervention by God that proclaimed to its witnesses that death is not the final word, neither for Jesus nor for those who walk in Jesus' way.

Jesus' resurrection is consistently presented as good news for us. He is the "first [of many] to rise from the dead" (Acts 26:23), the "firstborn [the first of many] from the dead" (Colossians 1:18; see also Revelation 1:5). His resurrection holds the promise and the assurance of our own (1 Corinthians 15:1-28). Where formerly death was a fearful weapon in the power of the Enemy (Hebrews 2:14-15), now it is Jesus who holds the keys to Death and Hades (Revelation 1:18), who can close people in or let people out (Revelation 3:7). Jesus' path through sufferings and death to an indestructible life in God's presence becomes our path as well as we follow him (Hebrews 2:10; 6:19-20; 12:1-2).

DYING TO LIVE

Paul views our connection with Jesus as the God-given means by which we move from death to life. In Romans 6:1-14, Paul speaks about the Christian dying with Jesus now in this life as well as dying "in him" at the end of this life. The believer makes the transition to "newness of life" while still alive in the body, culminating in the experience of the resurrection from the dead later after physical death.

What does it mean to be "joined with Christ in his death"? Paul uses the experience of baptism to explain. This ritual often involved the immersion of the convert in a pool of water. Going into the water, the convert "died" to his or her old way of life; rising up out of the water, the convert stepped into a new way of life—a life that would be lived no longer for self or society but for God.

God's grace transforms this simple ritual into a mystical participation in Jesus' own death and resurrection. The convert is freed from the old ways of life by his or her "death" with Jesus; beginning to walk in newness of life, the convert has the assurance that this walk will lead to resurrection, as it did for Jesus. Attachment to Jesus in this manner opens up the way to

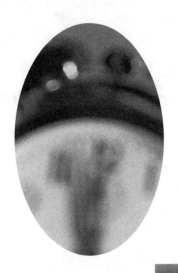

BIBLE

Dying to Live
Read Romans 6:1-14.
Visualize the process of baptism by immersion and the ways in which it symbolizes death and rebirth. To what have we been pronounced "dead"? Why? How will this show up in our lives? What does "walking in newness of life" look like in the real world?

Read Mark 8:34-38. What is Jesus trying to say, and how does Romans 6:1-14 help us? How are we driven to "gain the whole world," and why is this ultimately a path that leads to death? What wisdom do you take from Jesus' and Paul's challenges?

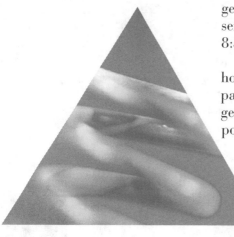

genuine life—losing one's "life" in one sense to find it in a truer sense (Mark 8:34-38).

Living beyond death is not without cost, however. Jesus and Paul tell us that some parts of us must "die" if we are to live a genuine and unending life beyond death's power to claim and constrain us.

Many people can quote Ephesians 2:8: "By grace you have been saved through faith." The larger context of this verse speaks of how God graciously brings people from death to life. Death is not an event at the end of life but a state in which people can live their whole lives. We are dead as long as we persist in the ways of living that displease God, that are "death-bound" for us, for our neighbors, for our whole society. Thinking of death not merely as a punishment for sin but as the consequence of sin can help us identify what is truly sinful in our own lives and in the world around us. What desires, drives, and attitudes lead to death or the diminution of life—whether for us or for others somewhere removed from us? The Scriptures consistently challenge us to see death not merely as an end or a punishment, but, ironically, as a way of life.

The same power that God put to work to raise Jesus from the dead (Ephesians 1:15-23) is put to work also "for us who believe," to liberate us from the power of this age (the death-bound life in which we are slaves to our human passions and experience God's wrath) and, ultimately, to experience God's kindness in the "ages to come" (Ephesians 2:1-7). God "made us alive with Christ" in a new way, beyond our physical but mortal life, beyond our deadness in sin.

CREATE What are the forces of death at work in our world? How are we involved in death-dealing and death-bound processes and systems—individually, as sub-groups, as a nation? Make a collage out of pictures gathered from magazines and Internet sites illustrating your answer to these questions, and then discuss each image and the collage as a group.

PAUL'S OWN TESTIMONY

Paul offers the reader many glimpses into his own struggles and experiences, always with a view to providing a living example of how to follow Christ (Philippians 3:17). In Philippians 3:7-15, Paul explains the way in which encountering Christ changed his estimation of his privileges by birth and his accomplishments, which had previously given him confidence about his life. He recognized that these things only gave him a false sense of security in the face of death, with the result that he began looking for the real answer to the transcendence, not the avoidance, of death.

That answer, he found, was seeking conformity with Christ's death, being shaped into the likeness of Jesus in his death as the path to life. As we become more like Jesus, particularly embodying the attitudes Jesus had as he set obeying God and serving others above his own self-interests (Philippians 2:1-11), we are assured that God will also make us like Jesus in the resurrection, since God will approve and reward our way of life (Philippians 3:20-21).

Paul also presents a negative example in those who "live as enemies of the cross of Christ," who serve themselves and their own appetites (Philippians 3:18-19), which Paul says is the way to destruction and the loss of the whole self in death. Christians are instead urged actively to "put to death" those facets of life that stand against God. To do so becomes the means by which loss of the whole self in death is prevented (Colossians 3:3-11).

BIBLE

Paul's Own Testimony
Read 1 Corinthians 6:9-11; Philippians 3:7-11, 18-19; Colossians 3:3-11. What ways of life, what values, what attitudes are identified as "death-dealing" or "death-bound" in these texts? What insights does this give you into these behaviors? Where do you disagree with the viewpoint in these passages? What are the positive alternatives to these behaviors and values? Why might these be more life affirming?

Name some of the death-bound attitudes or behaviors that have adversely affected your own life. With which are you currently struggling? What would change in your life if you "died" to those attitudes and behaviors and sought the alternative instead? How would this bring you closer to "living beyond death"?

LOOK CLOSER

What are the particular features of Jesus' mindset that Paul highlights in Philippians 2:5-11? What are some particular changes Paul wants to bring about in the relationships between Christians in the Philippian church (Philippians 2:1-4; 4:2-3)? How would the former enable the latter? How do other passages, such as Mark 10:45 and John 13:12-17, resonate with Paul's description of Jesus' attitude? How would following this example defeat "death-dealing" forces in our lives and our world?

NEW BIRTH, NEW LIFE

Another image biblical writers use for the "life beyond death" is new birth to a new life, a life not ending in death like our physical birth. First Peter draws out this image in some detail. Hearing and responding to God's invitation to life in Jesus brings about a new birth to a living hope that is characterized by all that this world's rewards and pleasures are not—unfading, imperishable, untainted (1 Peter 1:3-5). Since God's unfading word is the "seed" that gives us this new birth, this new life we live is "imperishable" (1 Peter 1:23-25; see also John 1:11-13). This birth gives us roots in the life beyond death (our inheritance is "kept in heaven"; 1 Peter 1:4); and beyond time (this inheritance will come "when [Jesus Christ] is revealed," for example, at the Second Coming; 1 Peter 1:13).

When John speaks of this new birth, he uses the language of being "born of the Spirit" (John 3:3-8), which indicates a personal encounter. Given the various ways in which the Spirit was believed to be present in the early church, early Christians understood the Spirit as a "holy Other" that came to them and interacted with them. The gift of the Spirit is of central importance for life beyond death. The Spirit's coming is linked with Jesus' triumph over death (Acts 2:24-33, especially verses 32-33) and connects us with that triumph and hope (Romans 8:10-11). It is the Spirit living within us that awakens us to real life and assures us of our redemption beyond this life (Ephesians 1:13-14; 4:30). The Spirit's

BIBLE

New Birth, New Life
Read 1 Peter 1:3–2:3.
How does the Scripture use the images of birth, inheritance, and "growing up"? What contrasts does the author create between our natural birth and the life, new birth, and possibilities that Jesus' resurrection has opened up? What are the motivators to invest oneself in cultivating the new life?

SMALL GROUP
Form teams of two or three. Make a list of the ways people might experience the presence and conversation of the Spirit as the "holy Other." Talk about any similar experiences you might have had. Tell about ways in which encounters with the Spirit can invite you to live more fully a "life beyond death."

MUSIC
Locate in your church's hymnal several hymns about personal holiness, rebirth, or the Holy Spirit. Which hymn appeals most to you? Why? What does the hymn suggest to you about living a new life or a "life beyond death"? What does the hymn suggest to you about God's presence? If you have time, sing a verse or two of the hymn.

presence in our lives is a sign of our new birth into God's family with an inheritance beyond mortality; it is also a constant summons to live out of that new birth, to keep walking in newness of life (Romans 8:12-17).

WALKING IN THE PATHS OF LIFE, NOT DEATH

First Peter continues to develop the image of new birth by contrasting two ways of life, two paths, open before the believer. One involves "the futile ways inherited from our ancestors" (1 Peter 1:18-19), which we are summoned to put behind us (1 Peter 1:14; 2:1). Those ways constituted nothing less than a slavery from which we had to be ransomed (1 Peter 1:18-19). The other involves the new ways of being, relating, and acting shown to us by God, the new Father into whose character and likeness we are invited to grow (1 Peter 1:14-16; 2:2-3). The latter path brings deliverance from the death-dealing ways to which we naturally turn and to which our society naturally turns us.

One cannot follow both paths, since they lead in opposite directions. Paul introduces the images of flesh and Spirit here to denote the guiding principles for the two paths. By "flesh" he means the natural inclinations of humanity apart from God; by "Spirit," he means the inclinations planted in the human mind and heart by God's indwelling Spirit. Those who cater to the former plant a harvest of death for themselves and nullify their hope of entering

BIBLE

Walking in the Paths of Life, Not Death
Read Galatians 5:13-26; 6:7-10, and "Bible 101: Flesh and Spirit." What do these passages reveal about the flesh? Why are the individual and collective works of the flesh incompatible with life in God's kingdom? What characterizes the new life and new community called into being by the leading of the Spirit?

CREATE

Make a diptych. Form two teams. One team will paste or sketch images that show the character and destiny of a life lived from the flesh on a sheet of poster paper. The other team will paste or sketch images that show the possibilities and fruit of the Spirit-led life on a second sheet of poster paper. Attach or hinge the two posters together to create a diptych. Display in a prominent area, and talk about what the diptych suggests about daily life.

Paul's language of *flesh* (Greek, *sarx*) and *spirit* (Greek, *pneuma*) has been taken to mean that the body itself is evil or sinful, while the soul "trapped" inside it is good. This is not what he means at all. After all, the body is targeted for redemption just as much as the soul. God has purchased all of us, including our bodies, which can now be used to glorify God (1 Corinthians 6:19-20). The life-giving Spirit promises life to our bodies in the resurrection from the dead (Romans 8:11; 1 Corinthians 15:35-49).

Rather, Paul uses the language of flesh to name everything about us that rebels against God, that resists transformation into the image of Christ, that seeks its own gratification. Our bodies are not our spiritual enemies, but our self-serving, self-gratifying nature is. "Spirit" (*pneuma*) combines the ideas of "breath," "wind," "spirit being." The resonance with God breathing life into Adam (Genesis 2:7) and with the Holy Spirit that moves where it wishes, like the wind (John 3:3-8), is strong. Paul uses it to refer to the Holy Spirit, breathed into us by God to empower and to guide our transformation. It is not our "reason," our "mind," or our "soul," but a God-given faculty that invites us to follow into a life beyond death.

SMALL GROUP

Form teams of two or three. Name some of the futile ways, the empty or hurtful attitudes, ambitions, and behaviors that you learned from your natural parents or guardians. How have these affected your adult life? What are some of the futile ways you have inherited from the values and patterns of the society around you? Of which do you most desire to repent? Pray for one another.

Close
Read 1 John 2:15-17; 3:14-15 aloud. Meditate on these verses in silence. If desired, pray: "Life-giving God, continue to show us the ways that lead to death and nothingness, and point us to the ways that lead to life. Help us let go of familiar but life-draining responses and pursuits. Open up for us the newness of life you promise in Jesus. Amen." Sing the chorus "Spirit of the Living God, Fall Afresh on Me" or another hymn about the Holy Spirit.

God's kingdom. Those who live in line with the latter plant a harvest of life and confirm their hope of entering the kingdom of God (Romans 8:12-17; 1 Corinthians 6:9-11; Galatians 5:13-25; 6:7-10; Ephesians 5:5).

LIVING THE AFTERLIFE NOW

The afterlife begins in *this* life through our rebirth by God or our mystical participation in the death and resurrection of Jesus. Eternal life begins as we live out a new set of inclinations and values, given to us by God's Spirit. In God's Spirit we live beyond the power of death to pervert and nullify our lives. Although we are still subject to physical death, a continuity of life continues between our coming alive to and in the spirit of God and the life we will continue to experience beyond death.

THE LARGER CANVAS

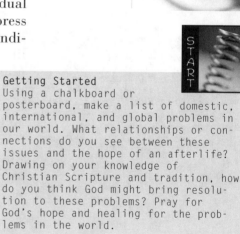

This session explores individual survival beyond death in the context of the broader dimensions of God's deliverance of all creation from death-bound systems and forces.

GETTING THE BIG PICTURE

So far we have focused on afterlife as a topic that mainly concerns individual people. The Scriptures, however, impress upon us the fact that the survival of individuals beyond death is merely one aspect of God's commitment to redeem God's whole creation and bring justice to the human sphere. In other words, this is not just "about me," but about God's interventions on behalf of all creation and against all the forces of death that mar the global community. Many of the topics normally associated with the afterlife—the resurrection of the dead, the Last Judgment, final rewards and punishments, heaven and hell—represent a small sampling of the topics commonly expressed by apocalypticism, a stream of thought in Judaism and Christianity that shows particular interest in the "bigger

Getting Started
Using a chalkboard or posterboard, make a list of domestic, international, and global problems in our world. What relationships or connections do you see between these issues and the hope of an afterlife? Drawing on your knowledge of Christian Scripture and tradition, how do you think God might bring resolution to these problems? Pray for God's hope and healing for the problems in the world.

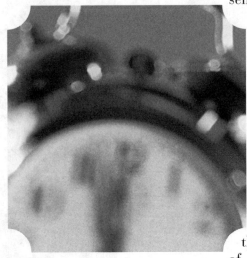

picture," or "broader canvas," that forms the backdrop for human existence. Apocalypticism looks into the primeval past and forthcoming future to make sense of the tensions and struggles of the present. It looks into the realm of God's throne and down into the infernal regions to make sense of everyday realities.

In the New Testament, the Book of Revelation is the most stunning example of an apocalypse. John's vision invites the reader to peer into the invisible spaces of God's throne room and the activity in the heavenly court, as well as to look into the abyss and the unseen places of darkness and the activities therein. John takes the reader back in time to the stirrings of angelic rebellion against God and forward to God's future restoration of all creation and all elements of creation to a state in which God's values are perfectly embodied everywhere. These visions help contribute to our awareness that physical life in this world is not the only, or the ultimate, reality.

Apocalypses insist that human life *and* death be seen against this larger backdrop and interpreted and evaluated in light of a broader vision of time and space. Although they can be misunderstood as escapist literature, apocalypses such as Revelation are very much concerned with the realities of this world. By presenting a God's-eye view and constructing a larger picture of the forces at work, apocalypses seek to put both the promises and pressures of society in perspective so that we can keep our focus on a greater and transcendent good and maintain our freedom from death-dealing systems.

Apocalypticism
Reflecting on events in the primeval past and forthcoming future and on the activities of otherworldly beings as a means of getting a larger perspective on the challenges and experiences of the present.

THE IMPORTANCE OF A BROADER PERSPECTIVE

A regular feature in one of the magazines I read as a child was a picture of some regular object or animal but taken from an extremely close-up perspective. For example, it would focus on the eye of a housefly or the vein of a leaf. It was often impossible for me to guess what the object was from the small portion the photographer had chosen to show until I turned the page to see the bigger picture.

I tend to walk around with my mind crowded with all the things I have to do, the problems that I am struggling to resolve—in short, locked into my own little world. Then I will take a trip in an airplane and look out the window. The number of houses and businesses multiply, the number of cars full of people full of their own concerns expand exponentially. I understand again where my concerns fit alongside the "grand scheme of things." I get a different perspective, and this quickly changes my outlook.

Getting the broader perspective makes a huge difference in knowing how to interpret the facts before us or discerning the significance of something we are involved in or making intelligent and faithful choices about our participation in something. We are concerned about a friend's secrecy and evasiveness only to discover in time that she was planning a surprise party for us. We enjoy wearing a particular brand of clothing until we learn the conditions of the workers who make the clothes. We are pleased with our investments in a particular multinational company until we learn of its disregard

BIBLE

Read Revelation 4:2-11; 5:6-14; 11:15-19; 21:1-8. Try to visualize these scenes and spaces. If you have time, form four teams. Each team will create a sketch of one of the Scriptures using markers and newsprint or poster paper. Show the sketches and talk about the following questions: Who is at the center of these scenes? How do they challenge your everyday focus? What feelings do these scenes evoke for you? What do these texts say about God's purposes for creation, especially for humanity? What light do they shed on our world as it now stands?

DISCUSS

A Broader Perspective
When has seeing the bigger picture shed new light on some particular situation you faced or on your general understanding of reality? How has this affected you, from the simple to complex choices? What about the biggest picture: How would an apocalyptic view of things shine new light on my choices and commitments here and now? Are you living wisely in light of the big picture?

for local ecology or its effects on foreign economies.

What the Scriptures say about "ultimate things" is so important because it can provide us with the most important of "big pictures," helping us to walk in line with what will be of value for eternity and not just for the moment "in our own little worlds."

THE GROANING OF CREATION

Paul perceived that the effects of sin were far reaching. Not only individuals, not only human society, but all creation was affected as God's creatures pulled away from God and gave themselves over to death-bound pursuits. In Romans 8:18-25, Paul speaks of creation itself longing for the time when God's redemption would come. Creation joins us in our groaning as we long for a life beyond the vicissitudes of this death-bound life, and we are invited to join creation in its groaning as it longs for release from decay, futility, and death. God's forthcoming interventions will bring freedom to all creation.

This vision has obvious implications for ecology and Christian witness. How many ecosystems have been destroyed, how many rivers and lands rendered toxic, by human greed and thoughtlessness? The environment has itself been turned into a death-bound system by the human element. Joining in this groaning is a means by which to remain free from falling into an easy complacency and cooperation with destructive, death-dealing systems and patterns.

However, there is more here than an ecological word. Creation itself has

BIBLE

Read Romans 8:18-25. On a piece of newsprint or a chalkboard, make a list of some indications of creation's subjection to decay, futility, and death. Which are beyond our control? Which can we do something about? What forces are making things worse, and where are there signs of concern and improvement? What should be our voice with regard to the care of creation?

How have you contributed, directly or indirectly, to the decay of creation? How have you or people you know been affected, in turn, by a nature that has been given over to corruption? What does this say about the circumstances of our life in this world and the challenges posed to affirming life? What connections do you see between personal tragedy (for example, coping with AIDS) and the groaning of creation itself? How does Paul speak a word of hope to all the situations you have listed?

become involved in spreading death and decay, whether through disaster or the proliferation of new diseases. Our personal pains and heartaches are part of a much greater cosmic heartache, crying out for deliverance from the only One who can bring it.

BABYLON, BABYLON

Rome proudly celebrated its achievements—its armies ensured peace and the rule of law, which in turn made trade and mercantilism prosperous and safe. Listening to the voices of the imperial court or local elites, one would think Rome was the gods' greatest gift to the world. John was listening to other voices as he looked upon Rome and penned his revelation. He heard the cries of men and women who were killed or enslaved while Rome was making its peace. John saw the despoiling of the provinces that resulted in luxury for the few elites and the poverty of those who were left out of Rome's prosperity. He watched as voices of protest were brutally silenced. He saw through the veneer of Rome's arrogant self-deification and the public image of Rome as a beneficent goddess and painted her quite differently—as the Great Prostitute, Babylon. Rome's relationship with the nations of the world was denounced as seductive defilement.

John gives a great deal of attention in Revelation to proclaiming God's judgment of death-dealing and death-bound systems (Revelation 17–18). God does not merely provide individuals with life after death. God acts against all the forces and incarnations of the power of death, including governments and whole empires that participate in the enslavement

LOOK CLOSER

Babylon, Babylon
Read "Bible 101: Apocalypses." Read Revelation 17:1-6; 18:1-24. Read 2 Esdras 11:36-46 and compare it to the passages in Revelation. Think about the kinds of policies, propaganda, and activities that characterize Babylon in these texts. How are these same practices expressed in contemporary political systems? Why do you think such practices recur in human systems?

How are you participating in, or benefiting from, death-dealing systems? How do you respond to John's challenge to "come out" from these entanglements?

CREATE

Make a collage or a drawing of images from our world that incarnate Babylon's death-dealing practices and values. Or you may choose to capture this in a poem, short story, or song. Just as Revelation presents New Jerusalem (Revelation 21-22) as an alternative to Babylon, you may wish to create a second piece that displays or celebrates what a life-making and life-affirming system would look like.

SERVE

Remember your discussion of ways in which "Babylonish" policies, practices, and propaganda may be at work around you (at the local, national, or international level), and identify a few that strike you as particularly important to expose and/or address. Investigate one of these more closely. What case can you make against its contribution to the diminution or destruction of life? How can you contribute to exposing or opposing these ill effects?

BIBLE

Witnessing to Life
Talk about Paul's attitude toward death and willingness to provoke the powers that be in 2 Timothy 1:8-14 and Philippians 1:21-23. Where are you with this? What in Paul's attitude challenges you or makes you more curious? What do his attitudes say to you about the reality and value of this life?

Eschatology
One's beliefs about how God will intervene in the future to triumph over all hostile forces, bring universal justice, and fulfill God's promises to God's people.

of humanity by death. God's justice is once again at issue. The death of faithful witnesses requires not only that they be given the reward of a life beyond death, but also that the system that killed them be held accountable as well (Revelation 6:9-11; 16:4-7).

WITNESSING TO LIFE

Trusting that God will grant life beyond death to God's faithful ones has empowered bold and courageous witness against death-dealing systems and practices throughout the millennia. Assurance that death was not the final word allowed, and continues to allow, individual witnesses to point other people to a different, life-affirming way, even in the face of brutal oppression. Here an important connection between individual afterlife and God's redemptive purposes for creation and for human community emerges.

Paul himself certainly made this connection. As he faced execution for his witness to the kingdom of God and the return of Christ in an empire that regarded such talk as sedition, Paul encouraged his younger colleague Timothy to continue that witness without flinching (2 Timothy 1:8-14). Jesus brought "life and immortality to light" (2 Timothy 1:10). Why, then, should people remain silent and cower before the repressive measures on the part of the death-dealing systems that act to protect and perpetuate themselves? Since Paul was sure that death meant being with the Lord, which he valued far more than anything in this life, he had nothing to lose and everything to gain by his bold witness (Philippians 1:21-23).

ESCHATOLOGY AND VALUES

One's *eschatology*—the technical term for beliefs about the end times or the transition from this age to the life of the world to come—should greatly affect one's values. We saw in the first session that people with *no* eschatology, viewing this life as the be-all and end-all of existence, might fall prey to a value system that promoted getting this world's goods and pleasures at all costs. The author of Hebrews, believing that this world is transitory and that an eternal life with God in an "unshakable kingdom" awaits the disciple (Hebrews 1:10-12; 12:26-29; 13:13-14; 2 Peter 3:10-13), promotes living always with an eye to keeping those eternal goods secure. The pleasures or advantages of sin, of not walking faithfully in line with Jesus' teachings and God's commandments, are always temporary (Hebrews 11:25). To give up everlasting honor and joy for the sake of this world's goods would be to repeat the foolish choice of Esau (Hebrews 12:15-17; see also Genesis 25:29-34).

Read Hebrews 1:10-12; 12:26-29; 13:13-14; 11:24-26; 12:15-17. What do these texts say about this present world? Where is true value to be found? Take an inventory of the way you spend your time, energy, and money. What are your priorities? Are these consistent with what you hold to be your own deepest beliefs about this world and the next? What would you need to change to begin to reflect your beliefs more fully and authentically?

Bible 101: Apocalypses

Because of the popularity of works of fiction such as the Left Behind series, we may think of apocalypses as concerned wholly with predicting a future that was far distant from the times in which it was written. On the contrary, apocalypses were very much texts for their own times. Their authors sought to interpret the features of their own landscapes in light of what they knew about God's standards, justice, and promises, so that they and their readers could be faithful witnesses to God in those situations.

Two apocalypses written around the end of the first century denounce Roman imperialism. In addition to Revelation, Fourth Ezra (2 Esdras 3-14), a Jewish apocalypse wrestling with Rome's destruction of Jerusalem, boldly protests against Rome's use of violence to establish its peace, its unjust practices, and its self-glorifying arrogance (2 Esdras 11:36-44). Here, too, God's justice demands that this empire be judged and removed, "so that the whole earth, freed from your violence, may be refreshed and relieved" (2 Esdras 11:46). In this regard, both Revelation and Fourth Ezra are rightly considered protest literature, calling the faithful to avoid being taken in by the system, to name its evils for what they were, and to live in line with God's values in the midst of that system however difficult that would be.

Eschatology and Ethics

Read 1 Thessalonians 5:1-11 and Romans 13:11-14. What are the connotations of sleeping or intoxication as metaphors for the way a person lives? To what degree are you sleeping or watchful for Christ's coming in triumph? What worldly intoxicants muddle your spiritual and ethical sobriety? How do the images you have studied of God's redemption of creation, judgment of human systems, and provision of life beyond death offer liberation from the stupor?

CLOSER Using a concordance, look up Bible verses speaking of holiness and justice. You may also wish to consult Bible dictionary entries under these headings. What does a life of holiness and justice look like? How does this image connect with the discussion of "walking in the paths of life" from the previous session?

Close
Tell about one or two things that have emerged from your study that really spoke to you. Pray for one another that the seeds sown will bear fruit in the weeks ahead. Close by singing the hymn, "O Day of God, Draw Nigh" or "O Day of Peace, That Dimly Shines."

ESCHATOLOGY AND ETHICS

One's eschatology has the potential to affect profoundly one's ethics. For Paul, the conviction that Christ would return for judgment and deliverance must lead Christians to use their lives differently from other people (Romans 13:11-14; 1 Thessalonians 5:1-11). Indeed, the privilege of knowing God and God's future interventions carries with it the responsibility of living differently—being alert to God's values and agenda in the midst of people asleep to God, sober and sensitive to God's evaluation of what is going on around us in the midst of people intoxicated by nationalism, consumerism, militarism, and the like.

The author of Second Peter describes the fiery destruction of this present earth and heavens and the hope of the promised "new heavens and new earth" where righteousness is at home. In light of this, the passage pointedly asks, "What sort of persons ought you to be?" (2 Peter 3:10-13). If we know the bigger picture, the text suggests, we will act wisely in light of this bigger picture. This wise response is encapsulated in the concepts of holiness and justice, two key scriptural images for the kind of life that pleases God, since they most reflect God's character.

Our focus in this session on apocalypticism and eschatology shows us once again that the more we think about final things, whether at the end of our life or at the end of history itself, the more we are asked to reflect on how we are living our lives *now*.

THE DAY OF THE LORD

This session explores the image of the Last Judgment and its implications for our daily lives.

THE CLIMAX OF HISTORY

The previous session was devoted to looking at the big picture of which individual survival after death is but a part. A central and climactic landmark in almost every apocalyptic vision is a day of judgment on which God or God's Messiah brings life in this world to an abrupt halt and evaluates everyone who has ever lived. The Messiah judges whether their lives were good or bad, whether they should enter into eternal life or perpetual death. Judgment becomes the principal image by which God's justice and God's sovereignty over creation are expressed and affirmed. It also becomes a principal motivator for adhering to the radical way of life taught by Jesus and inscribed in Scripture.

Getting Started
Check in with one another and pray for any concerns. Ask: What do you know about the image of Judgment Day? Do you think there will be a Day of Judgment? Why or why not? Do you think human history keeps rolling on without any final intervention and accounting on God's part? Why or why not? What are the implications of your response? What connections do you see between a judgment day and living an authentic Christian life?

KARA, AHMED, TISH, AND BRENT

Kara, Ahmed, Tish, and Brent

Read the conversation of Kara, Ahmed, Tish, and Brent. With which viewpoint do you find yourself most inclined to agree? Why? What merits do you find in the other positions? what weaknesses?

Kara: I've always tried to do what's right, not hurting other people and stuff. I was brought up Christian, but I've learned some neat things from my friends who are Buddhist, Zen, and New Age. I take whatever I think is true and try to live by it. That's working for me.

Ahmed: I have been a Muslim from my birth, and I have always done my best to observe its requirements. I believe it's made me a good person, an honest person. Some Christians came to my door and said I would go to hell. I replied that, however much they might think so, I know the God I've served from my youth will honor the way I've lived.

Tish: I always thought I was a good person. You know, compared to people who deliberately hurt others or don't care. But I also know I've done, said, and felt some pretty hurtful things. Since taking Jesus and church seriously, though, it's like there's someone else living inside me, helping me do what's right from the inside out. It's made me realize how far from God I really was before when I was just trying to be a good person.

Brent: I don't see what the big deal is. Christians have been waiting for two thousand years for Christ to return and judge the world. Hello! Wake up! That stuff is from an antique age when fear and religion kept people in line. We know better now. Live your life, be true to yourself, obey local speed limits, and you'll be fine.

THE CHRISTIAN VISION OF JUDGMENT

Almost every New Testament voice—beginning with Jesus—witnesses to the belief that God will judge the world. A time has been set when life as we know it, what the biblical authors call "this age," will come to an end. The Judge and his angels will appear to all, the dead from every age will rise from the grave and join the living, the good will be separated from the bad, and rewards and punishments will be meted out accordingly. The just, who have chosen the paths of life, will enter into a new dimension of existence, the "life of the age to come," or the "kingdom of God" (see Session 7). The unjust that have chosen to live in the ways of death will reap the fruits of their lives as well (see Session 6).

The conviction that God is just, bringing justice both to individuals as well as to nations, played a large part in the development of the perception that our life extends beyond the confines of this mortal existence. That same conviction about a God of justice led naturally to the conviction that there would be a final judgment at the end of life and the end of history.

WHO IS TO JUDGE?

The idea of a last judgment runs counter to popular trends in ethical thought. It says that there are absolutes and that right and wrong are not determined by the individual or by consensus. It proclaims that moral authority is "out there," beyond us, and that we will be held accountable to the standards of Another whether we agree or not, whether we have accepted this Other's code as our own or not.

Most scandalous in this day and age, the image does not merely show God on the

BIBLE

Read Revelation 1:7; 11:15-18; 20:11-15; 22:12. What are the elements of John's vision of the Day of Judgment at Christ's second coming? What feelings do you see illustrated in each of the Scriptures? What feelings or thoughts do the Scriptures evoke in you? What is the significance of this vision for life in this world, from personal morality to national policies and systemic practices? If you wish, you may also look at Matthew 13:24-30, 36-43; 47-50; Acts 17:30-31; and 2 Corinthians 5:10 to gain a broader New Testament perspective on this image.

LOOK CLOSER

Download and print images of paintings of the Last Judgment from the Web, and mount these on posterboard. Or find several representations in full-color art books, and bring these in for the group to see. What do you see happening in these scenes? What emotions and thoughts are displayed on the faces in the scenes? What feelings and thoughts do they invoke in you? What do these scenes say about God, Jesus, and life in this world? Evaluate these pictures. In what ways do they adequately represent God's justice, and in what ways do they fall short?

MUSIC

Sing "Lo, He Comes With Clouds Descending." What images strike you from this hymn? What feelings or insights does it evoke?

judgment seat, perhaps to judge people by their diverse religious standards and traditions. Rather, the image places Jesus Christ on the judgment seat, holding the world accountable to God's revelation of right and wrong specifically and particularly *in Jesus*.

WHERE MY DESTINY AND COSMIC ESCHATOLOGY INTERSECT

The second coming of Christ, an event usually directly associated with the Last Judgment in the New Testament, is the place where the story of personal survival after death and God's redemption of all creation come together. For it is at the Second Coming that individual people will be raised from the dead. Paul comforts his converts in Thessalonica with this word, assuring them that they will be reunited with their deceased sisters and brothers in Christ at Christ's return. His assurance gives a distinctive hope to accompany Christian grieving (1 Thessalonians 4:13-18), since we know all such losses of relationships will be restored.

People often wonder what kind of body we are supposed to have in the resurrection. Will we look the way we do now? What about people whose bodies have been lost to disaster, predators, cremation, or the like? Paul believes that there is an essential connection between our physical body and the resurrected body but that they are as different as a seed is from a mature plant, as dull is from glorious (1 Corinthians 15:35-53). Beyond death, at the Second Coming, our essence will be "further clothed" with a spiritual body representing God's final victory over death and his elimination of death from God's creation (1 Corinthians 15:54-57).

BETWEEN HERE AND ETERNITY

A recurring problem arises at this point. Billions of people have already died; no general resurrection of the dead has taken place. Where are these people now? Early Christian authors are not always consistent on this point. Paul, who speaks most clearly about the future resurrection of the dead, also expects to be "with the Lord" as soon as he dies (Philippians 1:23). Jesus promised the penitent thief that they would be in paradise together "today," that is, upon their deaths on the cross (Luke 23:43).

The author of Fourth Ezra tried to resolve such divergent views by suggesting that people experienced a foretaste of their eternal destiny, whether good or ill, for a week following their deaths then entered into an unconscious state until the last day (2 Esdras 7:75-101). The author of Second Peter also speaks of places of "deepest darkness" as an interim place of punishment until final judgment, although this is mainly for the fallen angels (2 Peter 2:4, 17).

Between Here and Eternity
What happens when we die if our bodies await the second coming of Christ for resurrection? Are we conscious in the interim? *What* are we in the interim? What connections, if any, do you see between this problem and the way we experience time?

The fate of the soul and the earthly body remains a theological enigma. Which side one emphasizes often depends on the situation one faces. In the face of death (for example, at a funeral), we tend to emphasize "being with the Lord" right at death; in less urgent circumstances, any long interim between death and the end seems less problematic.

WHAT REALLY MATTERS?

The New Testament speaks of the Judge's intention to weigh what we have spoken in this life (Matthew 5:22; 12:33-37) and what we have done, giving recognition for good works done and punishment for evil committed (2 Corinthians 5:10; 1 Timothy 5:24; Revelation 20:12). We will be accountable for acts of charity and justice performed or withheld (Matthew 25:31-46; James 5:1-5). This is not merely a matter of legalism or of being judged by works. The Scriptures bear witness throughout to a God who enables what is demanded and who equips people for the righteousness that is expected. Another way of looking at the Last Judgment is that the Judge will inquire into how we have responded to God's provi-

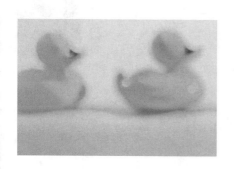

sions for life (Hebrews 6:4-8; 10:26-31; 2 Peter 1:3-11).

John Donne, poet and Anglican priest, said that "upon every minute of this life depend millions of years in the next, and I shall be glorified eternally or eternally lost for my good or ill use of God's grace offered me this hour" (*Sermons*, 3:13:514). One message of the judgment is that our choices and actions here really matter. It does not just proclaim fear—it gives significance to every moment of our lives. Every choice becomes an opportunity to choose life or death.

What Really Matters?
Read the Scriptures in "What Really Matters?" How are we judged? Do you think our judgment is just a matter of being a Christian? Why or why not? What is the connection between grace, moral action, and judgment in these texts?

Read the quote by John Donne. What does this say about the significance of each moment? Why should our choices, speech, and deeds matter so much? How would viewing each day, each hour, as Donne did change your focus and orientation? What would be different?

BE PREPARED (IT'S NOT JUST FOR SCOUTS)

Paul was especially concerned that his converts should live wisely and that they should be prepared for an ultimate accounting of their lives. Knowing that Christ would return as Judge, he models a wise response—living always with an eye to please the Judge (2 Corinthians 5:10) and giving the Judge his due service, which is nothing less than the life he gave for us (2 Corinthians 5:15).

The knowledge about Christ's return was thought to give the believer a tremendous advantage over non-Christians or nominal Christians. Expecting God's future intervention, one can use this life well, wisely, and without regrets at its end. As we saw in the previous session, this is the difference between being drunk and being sober, between sleeping and being awake and alert (1 Thessalonians 5:1-11).

Be Prepared
Form teams of two or three. Talk about the following questions: If Jesus were to return right now and begin the final judgment, would he find you prepared? What would he honor in your life? What would merit censure? What would you want to keep doing or change, so as to be more prepared tomorrow?

FINALLY—AN EXERCISE PROGRAM THAT REALLY PAYS OFF

LOOK CLOSER One of the many texts that talks about being prepared for the Last Judgment is the collection of Jesus' teachings found in Matthew 24:45-25:46. Read these Scriptures. Read about these Scriptures in *The New Interpreter's Bible* or another Bible commentary. What do the Scriptures say to you about Christian life and final judgment?

Our culture is caught in an exercise rage. Paul recognized its value but made a priority of training ourselves for godliness since this is of value not only for this present life (which physical exercise is good for) but also for the life to come (1 Timothy 4:7b-10). As an alternative to the proverbial rat race, the Christian heritage presents the race of faithfulness to God, which Jesus ran ahead of us and that we are now invited to run (Hebrews 12:1-2). Paul trained for this event by boxing—not the air, but his own inclinations and passions that ran counter to God's pleasure (1 Corinthians 9:24-27). Throughout his life, the goal of finishing the race honorably and successfully gave significance and purpose to every moment, keeping him focused and free from the distractions of the death-bound world (Philippians 3:12-16). Every victory over sin, self-deception, and misplaced confidence became not a laurel upon which to rest, but a conditioning of his spiritual stamina for the contests that still remained.

BIBLE

An Exercise Program That Pays Off
Read 1 Timothy 4:7b-10. How well are you conditioning yourself for the moral contests of life? Are you running so as to be crowned a victor on the Day of Judgment or so as to sit in the "penalty box"? Look at other texts speaking of the contest of life (Hebrews 12:1-4, 1 Corinthians 9:24-27; Philippians 3:12-16). How fully are you engaging these contests? Why or why not?

The gain? Paul approached his own death as one who lived prepared to die. He faced death with the gift of knowing that he maintained his integrity by keeping faith with God. He could therefore rest assured of God's keeping faith with him beyond death (2 Timothy 4:6-8).

CLOSE

Close
Read Revelation 22:12-13 out loud. Pray silently about this Scripture and about what it says to you today. Close by praying the Lord's Prayer together.

THE SECOND DEATH

This session explores the image of hell, the theological issues surrounding it, and its relevance for life in this world.

A HELL OF A PROBLEM

The idea of hell, a place of endless torment for sinful souls, strikes many people as a bit medieval. It was good for Dante and Milton, but maybe we have evolved in our thinking since then.

Curt: Doing bad things has consequences, but bad people usually get their just desserts in this life. Probably death will be the end of their existence forever, and they'll miss out on heaven. That would be bad enough, wouldn't it?

Jenna: God can work it out so that everyone is saved in the end. Maybe some will have to go through a kind of punishment to make up for their crimes or sins, but God will set a limit and let them into heaven eventually.

Darsey: I can't imagine how a loving God could torture people *forever*, no matter how bad they were in life. It's just not in God's character to be that vindictive.

Todd: We don't really know exactly how bad a sin is or how much harm it does.

> **Getting Started**
> Greet one another, and begin with prayer. You may create your own or use the following: "Lord God, as we wrestle with you today, and as we struggle to keep our grasp both on your love and your justice, reveal yourself to us anew; and keep us within the grasp of your grace. Amen."

Read the statements of Curt, Jenna, Darsey, Todd, and Riva. With which do you resonate most closely? Why? What are the merits and deficiencies of each position? What important issues or questions do they raise? What would be your own position coming into this session?

Form teams of two or three. Discuss the following questions. How much harm does a murder do? an act of adultery? a one-night stand? lying? How much punishment is appropriate? If these acts are acts against God and not just other people, how much punishment is fitting? Is punishing the wicked completely out of character with a God who is not only loving but also holy and just?

Not Everyone Sees a Bright Light

Have you ever had, or known someone who had, a near-death experience? What impact did that have on you or your acquaintance?

What landscapes have near-death experiences detailed, and how do they resonate with traditional pictures of the life after death? What are some different ways of accounting for this phenomenon? What is your view of such experiences?

Maybe it's far worse than we think, with far-reaching consequences we don't understand. An eternal hell might really be appropriate.

Riva: If people don't develop ethically and spiritually in this life, they have to come back after death and live life again and again until they get to a point where they are going to do the right thing.

NOT EVERYONE SEES A BRIGHT LIGHT

We often hear about "near-death" experiences and the reports that those who have drawn near the threshold of death bring back about bright lights, luminous beings, and reunions with relatives. Some of these returnees, however, have spoken instead of dark, fiery, thorny places, of being greeted with the sounds of weeping and anguish. It is especially interesting when such reports come from people who would not have considered themselves, nor been considered, religious, although, of course, they would have been exposed to the basic cultural information about the afterlife that we all share.

BIBLICAL IMAGES OF HELL

The Old Testament does not generally speak of after-death experiences. Isaiah may speak of an undying worm and unquenchable fire as components of God's judgment, but as a graphic description of the putrefaction and consumption of dead bodies (Isaiah 66:24), not an eternal hell. The intertestamental period (the centuries between the writing of the Old and New

Testaments, roughly 200 B.C. to A.D. 50)
saw the flourishing of interest in the places
of eternal punishment and reward, especially in the apocalyptic literature of the
period. This period often included "tours"
of these regions. The New Testament builds
on this heritage.

Surprisingly, Jesus, the friend of sinners,
says more about hell than any other New
Testament figure. One term he uses for it is
Gehenna or "the Gehenna of fire"
(Matthew 5:22, 29-30; 10:28; 18:8-9).

Voices from the apostolic period (the lifetime of Jesus' disciples) appear to express
somewhat different models. Paul tends to
speak in terms of "destruction" as the ultimate consequences of a self-serving, godless
life (Philippians 3:18-19; Romans 9:22;
2 Thessalonians 1:9; 2 Peter 3:7). "Anguish
and distress" happens on the Day of
Judgment "for everyone who does evil"
(Romans 2:9); Paul does not specify that
this happens ever after for them. The
Revelation to John, however, more than
makes up for Paul's reticence. Revelation is
full of references to perpetual punishment
after death. It is called "the second death"
(Revelation 2:11; 3:5; 20:4-6, 12-15; 21:8),
one far more horrible than the first. It is the

Biblical Images of Hell
Read several passages where Jesus speaks of punishment beyond death (Matthew 5:22, 29-30; 10:28; 13:41-42, 49-50; 18:8-9; 22:13; 25:41; Luke 16:22-24). What images does Jesus use to describe this experience? Look more closely at the context of each of these passages. What point is Jesus trying to make with each separate mention of hell?

What different images for the pun-
ishment of the wicked emerge from Paul and the author of Revelation? What merits are there to the view that the damned are simply annihilated at the judgment? How do Paul, Jesus, and John speak about this issue? Look closer at the passages in Revelation. What leads to experiencing the second death and what leads to escape from it? To what end is John using this language?

Bible 101: Gehenna
Gehenna is a place with a history. Before the Babylonian exile, when it was known as the Valley of Hinnom, it was a place of human sacrifice. Devotees of the cults of local gods would offer up selected sons or daugh-
ters as burnt offerings here. The prophets denounced the practices and pro-
nounced God's judgment on the place (Jeremiah 7:30-32). This image of horror obviously made an impression on the cultural memory of Judea, and *Gehenna* became a common term for the place of everlasting punishment, often involving fire.

Jesus also speaks of permanent exclusion from the Lord's presence (Matthew 7:21-23; 25:10-12; 25:41; 2 Thessalonians 1:9; Revelation 21:8), sometimes calling this the "outer darkness" where people will weep and gnash their teeth (Matthew 8:11-12; 22:13). He also speaks of the "furnace of fire" (Matthew 13:41-42, 49-50), of "eternal fire," and "eternal punishment" (Matthew 25:41, 46). People often draw attention to the topography of the story in Luke 16:19-31, but one should be cautious about making too much of the scenery in a parable.

CREATE
Seek out some images of hell. If you are artistically inclined, sketch or sculpt some representation of hell as you understand it.

LOOK CLOSER
Using the Web or art books, locate some of Dore's illustrations of Dante's Inferno, Bosch's hellscapes, and Blake's representations of hell. What do the images tell us about these places and the relationship of this life to the next? Why do they envision hell in the way they do?

death beyond death for those who refused to step into life beyond death in the here and now, as God invited them. The finality of death, however, gives no solace in Revelation, for it is further specified as the "lake of fire" in which God's opponents, whether human or angelic, are tormented "day and night without rest" (Revelation 14:9-11; 19:19-20; 20:7-10).

Post-apostolic writings (Christian texts from the late first and early second century A.D.), such as the *Martyrdom of Polycarp* (Chapter 11), seem to follow the "eternal fiery torments" model. The idea of endless torment for sinners after death seems to be an important concept in situations of martyrdom (see also the Jewish martyr text, Fourth Maccabees), as a motivator to endure brief torment now rather than break faith with God and as an assurance that the persecutors will meet the punishment their cruelty and hostility deserve.

WHY THE HELL?

Why should hell be part of the Christian landscape at all? Matthew 25:41 offers an interesting perspective (see also Revelation 20:10). Hell was not made for human beings originally but for the devil and his angels. Hell was a response, initially, to rebellion against God in the angelic ranks but came to be extended to other creatures (for example, human beings) who partici-pate in that larger rebellion through their own personal rebellions against God, using this life to promote the ways of death rather than to honor the Giver of life with one's life in this body.

Several early Jewish and Christian authors inquired into what good such final punishment of wrongdoers would serve. Paul, aware of the hostility and pressures that non-Christians have brought to bear on his fledgling congregations, knew that it would bring justice at last against those who had afflicted God's people, justice denied the contestants for faith during this life (2 Thessalonians 1:6-9). The so-called Apocalypse of Peter, a text from the early second century, carries this even further, stressing how eternal punishment would finally give satisfaction to those who had been murdered in this life. This author even portrays the victims (of homicide, infanticide, and abortion as well) as witnesses to the torments of their slayers.

Why the Hell?
What convictions about God stand behind the development of an eternal hell? What does the concept say about the seriousness of choices made in this life? How does the idea of hell help us grasp the seriousness of God's honor and holiness and the debt of obedience owed God by God's creatures?

Others regard hell as the necessary means by which God would vindicate his own honor in the wake of the many challenges and affronts to God offered by those who disobeyed God's commands or neglected God's gifts. The author of Fourth Ezra, a text that grapples with the justice of God, is horrified at the sight of the torments awaiting sinners. When he asks why the sins of a short life merit eternal punishment, he is told that it is not the gravity of the sin but the gravity of the One whose honor is despised that determines the length of punishment (2 Esdras 7:19-25, 37-38). John combines these two rationales in Revelation. The forces of open rebellion and defiance against God, seen in idolatrous, self-glorifying, violent, conspicuously consumptive nations, are judged for their crimes against God and their fellow humans.

MIDDLE GROUND

Christian tradition did not blithely or easily consign every sinner or non-Christian to hell (not that it is any human being's

63

prerogative to do so, anyway). Many pagans lived virtuous lives before Jesus came. Their only fault was that they did not come to faith in Jesus. But how could they help it? Would it be just for God to torture such people? In response to this came the doctrine of limbo, basically a pleasant place, neither heaven nor hell.

What about people who, though they believed in Jesus, lived sinful lives? Did their nominal commitment to Christ excuse a lifetime of bearing bad fruit? Was it just for God to condemn a more moral non-Christian to hell while letting an even less moral person into heaven just because she was a Christian? In response to this dilemma, the Roman Catholic Church teaches the doctrine of purgatory. This is a concept that emerged most clearly in the fourth-century church and that developed over many centuries. In purgatory, all sins committed by Christians during their lifetime receive their penalty, but gradually the soul is purged of its evils and attains heaven at last.

Middle Ground
Does our eternal destiny depend ultimately on what we do or on what (or in whom, for example, Christ) we believe? Divide the room into two halves. Ask people who believe what we do matters more to move to one half. Ask the people who believe that what we believe matters more to move to the other half. Why did you select the area you chose? What made it difficult to choose, if anything.

PERENNIAL QUESTIONS

Although a number of New Testament voices are loud and clear in proclaiming an eternal hell, Christian theologians throughout the centuries continued to wrestle with the nature, purpose, and duration of this punishment. Some of their leading questions were:

• *Is immortality a gift of God or something intrinsic to human nature?* Paul teaches that immortality is a gift from God for those seeking it through "patiently doing good," living this life to please God (Romans 2:6-7; 6:22-23). Why, then, would God give this to evildoers only to tor-

ture them forever? Or, being created in God's image, are we already immortal, so that annihilation is not an option?

- *Why would a good God torment people unceasingly for finite sins?* Some early church fathers decided that God set a time limit on the fires of hell. This position was ultimately rejected, since all sin came to be regarded as rebellion against the infinite God, thus meriting infinite punishment.

- *What would such torment serve, since it does not cure those who suffer nor can it provide an object lesson to dissuade others from sin (not after the Last Judgment, at least)?* Origen, a third-century theologian, tended toward the view that even hellfire was remedial. God's complete triumph meant that even the lost could not be lost forever. This position was also rejected by the church.

WHAT CAN HELL TEACH US?

We cannot be certain about the landscape of the eternal, invisible world. Jesus, John, and countless others have expressed a belief in a literal, eternal hell in which the damned are punished in a world without end. Many followers of Jesus have decided that an eternal hell is (forgive the pun) overkill and out of character for God, opting instead for an annihilationist model. They believe that God will simply destroy, rather than endlessly punish, the unrighteous. Others, drawing on resources other than the Judeo-Christian Scriptures, have sought to create some model whereby everyone ultimately ascends out of the morass of sin and death to arrive at a blessed eternity. As with so many mysteries, we shall only know fully when we enter into the mystery.

Just Rewards
Use the case study "Just Rewards" at the back of the book to dig deeper into the question of how we are judged. Should the woman who tries to live charitably and justly but who does not particularly subscribe to a religion go to hell while the man who uses people to get ahead, destroys lives and careers, lies, cheats, and steals, but calls himself a Christian go directly to heaven? Why or why not? What are the ultimate standards by which we are evaluated by God in this life?

Perennial Questions
Form teams of two or three. Select and discuss one of the perennial questions listed in the main text. What are the issues raised by this question? What resources do you draw on to resolve the question? Do you stick with scriptural authority? How do you arrive at an answer?

Nevertheless, the voices of the New Testament have a lot to teach us about life in this world through their use of hell language and imagery.

• Getting on God's bad side is the worst thing you can do in any situation.

• Sin is *serious*. Temptations to do what would not please or honor God must be resisted at all costs. Jesus used the hyperbole of cutting off body parts rather than sinning as an expression of the importance of getting out of sin's way (Matthew 5:27-30; 18:8-9).

• The forgiveness God offers us in Jesus is a great gift not to be missed. This lays upon us, however, the obligation of forgiving others as we have been forgiven, being committed to restoring relationships rather than satisfying our personal honor and outrage (Matthew 18:23-35).

• Loyalty to God is the highest priority (Matthew 10:28). Honoring God and keeping faith with Jesus are values never to be breached (Revelation 14:12), more important than indulging our desires, comforts, or preferences.

• Throughout Revelation, John especially uses the image of hell as a mental construct to help Christians overcome the challenges to faith and perseverance in the way of discipleship—whether it be the challenge of moral integrity in each new decision, the call for non-participation in and brave witness in the midst of a society that stands against God's purposes for human community, or the challenge of investing this life wisely.

Even if we remain unsure about eternal hell, taking its lessons to heart can strengthen our commitment to living with another and for one another as God intended and honoring the Giver of life as the enjoyment of life requires.

SMALL GROUP

What Can Hell Teach Us?

Form teams of two or three. Consider the life lessons communicated by New Testament authors speaking about hell and punishment after death. Talk about challenges you have been facing in your own life and that have been emerging as a result of this study. What images of or teachings about the eternal consequences of our life choices strike you as particularly authentic? How do they help you find clarity and guidance for the specific challenges you are facing?

Close

Reflect in silence on what you have learned during this session. Close with the following prayer: "Loving and Righteous God, please lead us into all truth concerning the difficult questions we have asked. Keep our hearts always focused on pleasing you, and help us renounce all destructive and hurtful behaviors that separate us from the fullness of life you desire for us. Amen."

THE LIFE OF THE WORLD TO COME

This session examines the biblical images of the community of the redeemed in eternity and the relevance of these images for living as witnesses to the Christian hope.

IMAGES OF HEAVEN

What is heaven like? Answers to this question are almost as numerous as the individuals answering it, suggesting that each of us views heaven in a unique way, highlighting aspects of hope that are especially important to each individual. Some expectations might include:

- a beautiful garden
- a shining city
- a vast and lavishly furnished mansion
- a dimension unlike any earthly experience or place
- a great reunion of family and friends
- a festive banquet
- an endless hymn of worship around God's throne
- a community perfect in peace, love, and joy

Getting Started
Check in with one another, and invite any follow-up insights on the topics discussed in the previous session. Read the list of the images of heaven. Tell about your images of heaven. What do you think it will be like? What do you count on seeing or having there? What will not be there? What does your image of heaven tell you about what is really important to you?

START

CREATE
Using any artistic medium (graphic, written, plastic, musical), create an image of heaven reflecting what you would view as a central component of the quality of life and human community enjoyed there. Tell the group what it communicates to you and how it helps you look at this life differently.

- a place where all questions are answered
- a place where all sorrows are resolved
- different for every person
- every person living harmoniously in a common vision

SOME IMAGES FROM THE BIBLE

In the Gospel of John, Jesus speaks of heaven in terms of a house with many rooms. Jesus' departure to heaven at his ascension is interpreted as his going to prepare a place for his followers in God's house, with the intention of returning to lead them back to himself (John 14:1-6). What this image emphasizes about life beyond death is that it involves intimacy with God, with Jesus, and with the community of disciples. Having been made part of God's family by Jesus, we are all brought to live at home with God at last and to enjoy his love and presence forever.

The author of the Letter to the Hebrews uses several images for that "undiscovered country." One image is a heavenly temple, of which the Jerusalem Temple was a stony imitation (Hebrews 8:1-2, 5; 9:11-14). This image also highlights the fact that heaven is all about entering God's real presence in all its fullness and glory, knowing God and having access to God in a way that is only hinted at in this life. Hebrews also speaks of a "homeland" and a "city," a place where disciples will have a permanent home—one that cannot be taken away from them, and one that is not temporary and destined for an end like their native lands here (Hebrews 11:8-10, 13-16; 13:13-14). Heaven lies beyond the material, physical creation, not merely "up in the sky," and has a distinctly different quality: It is lasting, permanent, abiding.

The readers of the Letter to the Hebrews had suffered significant losses on account of their Christian commitment. They no longer felt at home among their disapproving neighbors and families and needed to be insulated against *wanting* to feel at home again in this world. Wanting to belong *here* would lead them to betray the commitments that would allow them to be at home *there*, in God's eternal presence. The author also wanted to assure them that the good things God has prepared for his faithful ones far outweigh any earthly possessions or comforts they might lose or be asked to forgo. Keeping their hearts fixed on eternity would enable faithful perseverance.

The Revelation to John presents a very detailed description of heaven—a city, New Jerusalem, that comes from God's realm and takes its place upon a new earth (Revelation 21:1–22:5). Its perfection and grandeur are merely a reflection of the One who dwells in its midst. Indeed, there is no temple in heaven because God is fully present everywhere. The perpetually open gates signify that there are no longer any threats to the peace and safety of its inhabitants, no dangers against which to bar the doors. Those who oppose God's ways will never come near to disturb that city.

Depicting unseen realities in such detail serves to make them all the more real and present to the early readers of these texts. All three texts assume that the faithful disciple will face hostility and loss in this life on account of his or her confession of Jesus and commitment to a distinctive set of values, hopes, and behaviors. To sustain them on the road, these voices seek to keep the end of the journey in clear view, real, and worth the struggle.

DISCUSS

How real is heaven to you? How willing are you to forgo earthly enjoyments for the sake of attaining some invisible, future paradise? When have you been challenged to do so? How did you respond to the challenge?

How do images of heaven affect what we value and look for in this life? For example, if heaven is about enjoying the presence and love of God forever and fully, does this mean that we make more opportunities to enter into God's presence here on earth?

HEAVENLY BODIES

What will we *be* after our body is gone? Paul, as we saw earlier, is insistent that we will be "embodied" in some sense (1 Corinthians 15:35-57). We will continue to have a personal existence, one that is somehow connected with the person we have been here. In a later letter to the same church (2 Corinthians 4:16-5:10), Paul talks about life in this body being a partial clothing or a dwelling of our person in an inferior tent. After death, however, we are not left unclothed or naked by the loss of this body, but rather go on to be fully clothed, coming to live in a new body that is an "eternal tent." For him, our "person" is in effect that which is housed in one kind of body or another, not identical with the body itself. All that we know of mortality in this body—all that makes us "groan" as we run into our physical limits and as we lie vulnerable to attack in this body—will be swallowed up by life and immortality in the life beyond.

Paul never leaves metaphysical discussions without practical, ethical conclusions. Since he has the hope of being with the Lord through eternity, Paul has a single-minded focus in this life: to please the Lord in all things (2 Corinthians 5:9-10). This gives him integrity in all he does. Since it is his inner person that survives for eternity and that provides the greatest constant between this life and the next, Paul realizes that it is not the outer person that matters in terms of form, beauty, attention, and energies, so much as the inner person. This gives him courage in the face of the hardships he endures in the body for the sake of responding faithfully to God's call, as well as a clear set of priorities when faced with costly decisions.

BIBLE

Heavenly Bodies
Read 2 Corinthians 4:16-5:10. What images does Paul use to compare life in this body with life after death? What is the relationship of who you are to the body people can see? What is their relative value in light of eternity? How does Paul's view of who we really are help him and his readers embrace hardship and loss for the sake of obedience to God? How does this help you prioritize your placement of value and investment of energy when it comes to who you are? How do you think Christian communities can better reinforce these values?

ΜΑΤCHES ΜΑDE IN HEAVEN

What kind of relationships will we have in heaven? Will we still exist as family groups? Will we still be married, single, or divorced?

Trying to stump Jesus, some rivals devised a strange case study for him. A woman had seven husbands in succession in this life. Who would be her husband in the next life? (Matthew 22:23-33; Luke 20:27-40). Jesus declares the question invalid, since life in the next world does not carry on in the same way as it does here. There is no more marriage, since there is no more death (and no more need for procreation, a primary purpose for marriage in the ancient world).

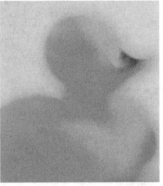

For us, however, marriage is not merely about procreation but about companionship, intimate knowledge and love of one another, the sharing of life's joys and sorrows. Is this lost in heaven? Marriage is also about exclusive attachment, about bestowing on another person a level of love and commitment that is withheld from other people. Family also marks boundaries and different levels of love and commitment offered to "family" and "not family." In heaven, God's vision for all human relationships becomes a reality—the vision of a person loving all others as himself or herself in the greater family of God. In effect, all people enjoy with one another, and in God, the kind of soul mate intimacy and community that marriage or family, at its best, merely prefigures in this life.

BIBLE

Matches Made in Heaven
Read Luke 20:27-40. Why would marriages not continue past death? Why might such exclusive, boundary-forming relationships be out of place? What does this say about heaven? Is it a place with less love or more love than earth with its marriages?

WHAT IF SOΜEONE I LOVE IS NOT THERE?

Serena: I can't buy this heaven and hell thing. My sister isn't a Christian, though she's

Read Ephesians 2:11-22. If in heaven God's vision for human community will be made real, does that mean former slaves and slave owners will be united in love? ex-POWs and their captors? the descendants of Holocaust survivors and the descendants of their murderers? If heaven means complete reconciliation with our enemies, who do not happen also to be God's enemies, what might this say about the quest for reconciliation in this life? Why should we pray for enemies now?

STUDY **What If Someone I Love Is Not There?** Read the conversation between Serena and Curtis. With whom do you identify more? What are some of the strengths and limitations of each perspective? How would you answer the dilemma posed by Serena?

More Than a Place Read the Scriptures cited in "More Than a Place: A Quality of Life." What is the significance of each of these facets of the life of heaven? What does each say about life here and life there? For whom would these images of the quality of life in heaven be especially important in the first century? in the world around us? Which of these images or longings resonates for you the most? Why do you find this an especially important component of the Christian vision of eternity?

a good person. Is she going to heaven? How could I enjoy heaven without my loved ones?
Curtis: Wouldn't it be enough to be surrounded by God's love and presence? I think, whatever regrets we might have, God's love will push that all aside.
Serena: I don't believe anyone can make you forget someone you love. Besides, if she's not there, I think I'll be angry with God.
Curtis: Who knows how differently things will look in heaven? Perhaps your sister's decision not to honor Jesus and follow him will look a lot more like rebellion. Perhaps sin will seem a lot worse from the perspective of experiencing God's honor, holiness, justice, and love. I notice, by the way, that you're pretty sure you'll be in heaven!

MORE THAN A PLACE: A QUALITY OF LIFE

In addition to providing images of heaven, New Testament voices say much about the quality of that existence.

• a place of rest where our labors to make a positive contribution and our struggles against the wrong around us and our own inclination to sin will come to an end (Hebrews 3:7-4:11; Revelation 14:13)
• a homeland, a place of belonging (Hebrews 11:13-16)
• a place of permanence where we will no longer suffer the loss of the good things we enjoy nor the insecurity that that brings (Hebrews 10:34; 13:13-14)
• face-to-face encounter with, and enjoyment of, God and of Christ
• the healing of all the sorrow and pain, the mourning and loss, endured in this life, the effects of death being undone by God's love and care
• a place for the healing of the nations after a history of war, strife, and enmity

- a place where all live by the light of God (Revelation 7:9-17; 21:1–22:5)
- a new order where justice is at home (2 Peter 3:13)

Some of these hopes or promises emerge from the biblical authors' awareness of what is *not* right about life in this world. Hopes for the world to come are often born from criticisms of life in the present order, the sense that something is out of order *here* with God's desires for human community and the rest of creation.

PIE IN THE SKY?

Heaven has often been misused as the hope for "pie in the sky in the sweet by and by" to keep people of little means, or even people living in oppressive socioeconomic circumstances, content with their lot, and to defuse any reformist or revolutionary energies. Sociologists of religion have frequently noted the correlation of a belief that heaven will give us everything we lacked in life with a tendency not to give concerted attention to addressing social ills. And, of course, Karl Marx is remembered for his famous (infamous?) critique of religion's role in maintaining the status quo. As "the opiate of the people," it siphoned off any creative energies that might otherwise have come from discontent.

In the life of the early church, however, visions of God's reward for the faithful disciple encouraged bold witness of a vision for human community in which all were valued as God's creation and daring critique of a social and political order that failed to enact God's desires for human community and global stewardship. Such visions enabled disciples to live an alternative vision for human community, often in the face of significant censure and opposition.

DISCUSS

Pie in the Sky?
How might the view of heaven as an opiate for the masses or as a compensation for what one does not have now affect one's view of daily life? What are the effects of using religion this way? How might the visions for life in the world to come shape our life before death more positively? How might they shape what we work to realize in human community? How might they prioritize our efforts and goals in this life? How might they move us to witness in this world?

CLOSE

Close
Sing or read the hymn "My God, I Love Thee, Not Because I Hope for Heaven Thereby" (originally a Spanish poem attributed to Francis Xavier). As a group prayer, invite everyone who wishes to offer thanks to God for something they have discovered or some change that has happened in the course of this study. Ask God for continued growth in, or clarity about, some aspect of this study. Close by greeting one another with the following words: "May the peace of Christ be with you."

CASE STUDIES

Getting Started

Use any of the following case studies as vehicles for digging further into issues raised by the sessions or as tools for getting discussions started.

High Anxiety

Jonah usually did not think twice about boarding an airplane. As with so much in our world, all that changed after the events of September 11, 2001. Two months after those events, Jonah was scheduled to attend a conference in Denver. His wife, Mary, had been expressing her reservations about his flying throughout those two months, while he assured her that he would be all right and that they had to move forward with their lives in faith not fear.

To help assure her, he reminded her of how God had looked out for him over a decade before. Jonah was driving home after midnight, approaching a familiar intersection a mile from his home. The light was green, and he was inclined to "make" the light. As clearly as if spoken from the back seat, he heard a voice say, "Stop!" As he abruptly halted at the intersection, a car went speeding downhill through the red light. A collision had been averted. "When it is my time, I can't avoid my death; until it is my time, I won't fear death."

When the week came, however, Jonah began to wonder if this would be his time. He asked friends to pray for his safe return. He wondered if he had already accomplished his purpose, perhaps simply in siring his three children. Was God done with him? The day before flying, he wrote letters to his wife and each of his children, affirming his love for each of them and giving any necessary parting information, words of encouragement, and apologies. He was surprised to find himself crying. He flew out, enjoyed a productive conference, and returned home without event. Since then, he has been much more open with his wife and rarely refuses an invitation from his children to play. The fear was without foundation, but the lessons he learned about what was really important to him were a new foundation.

• Is God personally involved in our life and death? Does God have a time for each person to die? Can we avoid death by changing our travel plans?

• Why does the possibility of death make us so afraid? What are we so reluctant to lose? How does this help clarify what we hold to be of value?

• How was flying or not flying a faith issue for Jonah? Was he correct to oppose faith to fear?

• Why did Jonah respond to the possibility of death the way he did? Why was it important to him to write those letters? Why was it important to him to go to the conference, even though it might expose him to greater dangers than staying home?

• Have you ever seriously confronted the fact that you would die? That you might die imminently? How did you respond? What were you prompted to do? What did the experience tell you about how you were living your life and where your highest priorities were?

Ghost Story

A husband and father left his house on a business trip wearing the new trench coat his wife bought for his birthday. While on the road, a tractor-trailer failed to brake behind him and crushed his car, killing him instantly. That night before she got the call, his wife felt his presence in the living room where she was reading. Turning, she thought she saw a faint image of him standing there in his trench coat. The experience was strangely familiar and comforting rather than alarming.

Later that night, the highway patrol called. She immediately telephoned her son, who was away at college. As they shared their grief, the son told his mother that somehow he knew something had happened to his father. A few hours before, he thought he felt his presence in his dorm room. He looked around, and when he looked at the window, he thought he saw a shadowy reflection of his father in the glass. The son remarked: "It was a little weird. It looked like he was wearing a trench coat, but Dad doesn't own one, does he?"

• Does this story strike you as true or plausible? Why or why not? Does anything in your experience resonate with the experience of this mother and her son? This should be a safe place to tell your "weird stories" and process them with the group.

• What happens to a person when he or she dies? Is there a time of transition when he or she is "available" to people still living? Does it make a difference if a person's death is anticipated or sudden?

• What is the "ghost's" intention in visiting his wife and son? What effects—immediate and long-term—might this have on them?

• Why might the wife and son "see" the deceased at the time of his death? Could the son's experience be psychologically manufactured?

Just Rewards

Kelly worked as a service technician for an aviation company. She was not brought up in the church and never became particularly religious. If there was a God out there, he did not seem to cut her any breaks. Having ended a marriage to an alcoholic that had turned abusive, Kelly found herself struggling to make ends meet and provide a reasonably secure life for her two kids. She loved them very much and at the end of a hard shift always gave them the attention they needed as if she had just gotten up from a good night's sleep. Kelly tried to treat people with kindness and help others out where she could, perhaps in part because she knew how hard it was to keep your head above water when others keep trying to shove you down.

Scott made a six-figure salary working for a mergers and acquisitions firm. He went to church with his family and was "born again" when he was thirteen. However, he was also a shrewd and practical businessman. He was working on a project to consolidate some airlines and their support networks. To get the respective boards to agree, he made assurances about retaining personnel and pensions and the like. Once the deal was done, he followed his directives to liquidate a number of the companies and all their assets to maximize the profitability of the new conglomerate, getting a nice bonus on the deal. Kelly found herself out of work and close to being out of a home.

In one of life's little-noticed ironies, both were killed by drunk drivers three weeks later on New Year's Eve.

• What do you think will happen to Kelly and to Scott on the other side of death?

• Does our eternal destiny depend ultimately upon what we do and how we live toward other people or upon what we believe (for example, "receiving Christ")?

• If both belief and right action are important, what happens to the person who has one but not the other? What happens when our actions are mixed or our beliefs uncertain?

• What value is it to be "born again" or "receive Christ" if a transformed life is not also the result?

SERVICE LEARNING OPTIONS

IDEA #1: Attend a funeral

You have probably attended several funerals by this point in your life. Perhaps sometimes it was for a person so close to you that you were dealing mainly with your own grief; perhaps sometimes it was a more perfunctory show of support for the grieving family. In the course of thinking intentionally about death and the life beyond death, however, attending to the services surrounding a death can trigger many new insights into our own mortality and the resources we have to find and offer genuine hope in the face of death.

Go to the wake and to the funeral of someone in your church or someone related to a colleague or a friend. Listen to the words that are spoken to the grieving or about the departed in both settings. Observe the way other attendees respond to the corpse, the family, the setting. Insofar as you are comfortable doing so, try to connect with and respond to the people around you and to those most affected by the loss.

What is remembered about the person? What connections with the deceased are remembered and celebrated? What do you want your legacy to be? Nothing can clarify what is important about a life like seeing what is left in the hearts and minds of those who remain behind.

IDEA #2: Set your house in order

Preparing for one's own death is both a very valuable, practical task and a transforming experience. It is also often a great gift to the family one will leave behind.

Using the standard forms that are legal in your state, prepare your will. As you do so, be alert to the emotions and realizations this process will evoke in you and, if doing it in conjunction with a spouse, together.

Make time to take care of unfinished business with family members and friends. What do you need to say to members of your immediate family or closest friends? What unresolved conflicts or hurts need to find reconciliation so that neither you nor they will have to live with regrets or unresolved conflicts when death intervenes in the relationship?

Plan your own funeral service. What message do you want to convey to your family and friends about life, death, and life beyond death through Scripture, song, and worship? Some excellent resources for this task would include the funeral services found in *The Book of Common Prayer* (which also includes lists of possible Scripture readings) or the sections of "hymns for funerals" in most hymnals.

IDEA #3: Care for the dying

Dying can be an isolating and lonely experience. One of the greatest gifts we can give is friendship and company for those who are crossing the final threshold.

Visit a patient in hospice care or another terminally ill person regularly. If you currently belong to a church, the pastor or visitation minister might be able to help connect you. Some things that might be helpful for the dying person would be to think about the good things he or she has done or enjoyed, share forgiveness, talk about how he or she has experienced God in this life, and what he or she looks forward to across the threshold. Be open, as well, to what your friend can bring to your life. Relationships such as these can be as encouraging for the caregiver as for the dying.

IDEA #4: Explore other views

Think together about other views or models of the afterlife within and beyond the Christian tradition (for example, reincarnation in Hinduism). What questions about this life do they seem geared to answer? What effects might they have on how one lives this life? What points of contact do you detect between these models (and their underlying rationales) and the models found in the Christian Scriptures? Where do they diverge and to what effect? If possible, carry out this project in conversation with friends of other faith traditions, so as to get an insider's perspective.